MW01128250

1

How to Teach Anything:
Break Down Complex Topics and Explain with Clarity, While Keeping Engagement and Motivation

By Peter Hollins,
Author and Researcher at peterhollins.com

Table of Contents

Chapter 1. Lessons from the Science of Pedagogy

Imagine you are with a friend who has asked you to show them how to do something that you're an expert in. They know nothing and need to be taught. How do you go about doing this? Most of us are more familiar with being in the shoes of the student and not the teacher, and when we're put on the spot like this, we're confronted with an interesting perspective: seeing knowledge from the perspective of the one who has to communicate it to someone else.

You probably had a few favorite teachers in school or university, but what exactly made them so effective? If you consider yourself a lifelong student and autodidact, you probably know that your theoretical approach, your attitude and your methods make all the difference. In this book we'll be looking at learning, but through the less common perspective of a teacher.

But rather than focusing on the philosophy of education in general or on school curricula, we'll be exploring the most fundamental underpinnings of what makes an excellent teacher, whether it's formally in the classroom or simply when helping out a friend.

The wonderful side effect is that mastering the role of an effective teacher has a way of making you a better learner, as you become familiar with learning and knowledge acquisition as a worthy subject in itself. We'll start with the foundations of *pedagogy*, or the study of education and learning. But hopefully, by the end of this book, you'll be able to use these general principles in creative ways that extend well beyond the standard teacher-student context.

Five Key Pedagogical Approaches

Teaching is in essence a kind of conversation, where new information is communicated and conveyed to a person who doesn't possess it. The approach you take depends on how you see the student, the teacher, the relationship between them, the information, and the rules governing the transfer of knowledge.

To teach your friend what you know, you could start with what they already understand, then build from there. For example, you teach a basic principle first, or draw on their existing knowledge of concepts, to expand and introduce something new. You strengthen this new acquisition by engaging in problem-solving tasks. Your role as a teacher is basically to lay out a useful obstacle course for your student, who, in moving through it, learns new things.

This is called a **constructivist approach**. This is a great way to teach complex ideas, and it works because it builds these major concepts up from smaller, simpler ones. The student masters these then moves on in a structured way. For example, students often learn an instrument in this manner—first master the scales, reading music and basic handling of the instrument before moving on to more and more complex combinations of those skills.

If you're teaching more than one person, say two friends together, utilize the constructivist approach by creating an environment of collaboration between the students. Instead of proceeding in a highly structured manner like some other methods, you use what they both know as the basis for how you go about relaying what you want to teach. Analogies are a particularly useful way to do this and allows students to "construct" an understanding of a new concept based on the old one.

However, one drawback of this approach is that it can be unstructured. Some students struggle to make connections between different concepts and just don't learn well that way. They require structure and would prefer to be told exactly how to think and understand something, rather than being expected to construct their own understanding of concepts. (McLeod 2019)

But you can take another approach. Did you ever sit in a classroom as a child, and wonder, "what's the point of all this?" because you couldn't understand how to apply the lesson to the "real world"? You wouldn't have thought so if your teacher had used what's called an **integrative approach**, i.e. teaching that embeds new knowledge in a practical, applied way. An example is a language teacher who has students role play certain encounters they'd likely have in a different country, like ordering food in a restaurant.

three books and ask them to devise a question they think best taps into the material contained in all three. This triggers them to not only seek solutions and new methods, but to even frame their own inquiries from the beginning.

While this method has many benefits, such as its unique ability to foster curiosity, it comes with some drawbacks. For one, it can be very difficult for a teacher to prepare for an inquiry-based approach. Exhaustively teaching a concept through a series of questions and answers takes much more effort than other approaches. The method can also fall flat if your students can't answer the questions you've prepared for them. In the worst case, it might even make them feel embarrassed and lower their confidence, especially if they have learning disabilities or aren't quick thinkers. (Gutierrez 2018)

If you're wondering whether these approaches can be blended, the answer is yes. The **reflective approach**, in fact, is one final pedagogical method that places regular reflection at the center of learning. Though all these approaches are valuable for different reasons, none will work if they're applied unthinkingly to inappropriate situations. Under the reflexive approach, the teacher regularly stops and appraises the techniques being used, and adjusts accordingly.

Is what you're doing actually working for this student, and this topic, in this moment? Why or why not? What would work better? Trainee teachers are often encouraged to stay in reflective mode as they themselves learn what is effective and what isn't, and why. This approach highlights an important principle: that teaching is practical—it's about what works. There are no topics too difficult or students too stupid, only methods that are unsuitable. When you take on the reflective perspective, you remind yourself that teaching is just a tool, and that you can and should try different approaches to reach your ultimate goal. This promotes experimentation, but like the inquiry-based approach, it demands a lot of effort from the teacher to devise strategies for teaching approaches that are new to them.

Everything in the chapters that follow refers back to one or more of these five pedagogical approaches, in one way or another. It's worth remembering that although much of the available theory on teaching and learning is designed for conventional classrooms, these approaches and methods are universal, and might be applied in the classroom. For example, does reducing cognitive load mean handing ready-made explanations to students so they expend as little cognitive energy possible, which they could use to form new schemas? This certainly would fly in the face of the experience of many teachers, who have found that providing partial solutions can be more effective. Another dilemma arises when considering the use of audio-visual materials. While these tend to reduce cognitive load when used sparingly, overdoing it can actually increase the cognitive burden.

Remember, though, that our aim in this book is not to devise more effective school curricula or philosophize about the teaching profession—rather, we are using these principles for ourselves, to become better teachers and facilitators in any learning endeavor. We can take the most obvious and powerful lesson from this theory: that learning, when it occurs naturally, is incremental and happens in small units that build on one another. Also, if we hope to teach to our best abilities, we need to find ways to mirror this natural learning process and support it in the people we're attempting to teach.

This means paying close attention to cognitive load—does your student have enough stored knowledge to draw on? Are you presenting too many things at once? How are you pacing the delivery of information, and is this overwhelming or gently challenging your student?

A related way of thinking about human learning is called the information processing model, where the brain is seen as a kind of computer. It begins with sensing and perceiving information, where we determine whether it's worth paying attention to. Then, we hold this information chunk in our short-term or working memory for a few seconds but, unless we commit it to long-term memory somehow, it more or less disappears.

The next step, if it happens, is the information is encoded and filed away in long-term memory in a mental schema, along with any cues to help with retrieval later on. The next step would then be retrieval, which is often triggered by a specific environment.

So how can we use this to become better teachers? Let's look at it through an example. Say you want to teach a group of people the benefits of using a certain product. First, you'll need to find ways to help this group retain the information in their **sensory memory**. As the name suggests, you do this by appealing to various senses, of which the most important are sight and hearing. To do this, show them the product and distribute some around so the group can touch and feel it. You should also explain the benefits of using it orally through words, as well as visually through infographics and other materials. Different people learn better when emphasis is placed on different senses. Using hearing, or words, will help some learn better, whereas others will respond to being able to feel the product in their hands.

Then, we need to ensure that sensory memory converts to **short-term memory**. Factors that influence this transfer are the amount of information that needs to be processed, the level of attention from the student, and individual cognitive abilities. Thus, if you can make the earlier step as interesting as possible to engage and gain the attention of your students, you'll activate their senses and help transfer their learning to short-term memory.

The final step is to take this information and commit it to their **long-term memory**. This can be tricky, but repetition is key. Find novel ways to say the same thing so that you can drill the most important bits into the minds of your students. Keep the information you're providing focused and break everything into small, digestible parts. Connect it to a real-life purpose. So, if you want them to sell the product, emphasize which benefits are most popular. If you want them to start using it, emphasize common problems and how the product will help solve them. All of this will help them retain the information in their long-term memory, ensuring they won't forget it for a long time to come.

Teaching tips from the cognitive load theory and the information processing model

Knowing about the brain's "architecture" and its procedural processes, we can optimize learning. According to John Sweller, we can process a maximum of two or three pieces of new information in our working memory at any one moment, and hold this focus for around twenty seconds. When we transfer something from working to long-term memory, we can be said to have learnt it. So, take your time. Break information into chunks and feed them into long-term memory slowly and steadily. Be explicit and detailed in your explanation. Provide plenty of examples, and link as many concepts as possible to those your student already possesses, so as to anchor them.

Other tips include taking a short break every ten or fifteen minutes, since attention often flags anyway. You could switch activities rather than stopping learning entirely. Just keep things fresh and moving. The goal is to keep your student engaged and active. Encourage conversation with questions and prompts (recall the inquiry-based approach), and mix things up. Since time and attention are limited, guide the process by showing your student what's most important and what they should focus most on.

Draw on long-term memory by connecting new material to old, contextualizing, inviting deeper thinking about the topic or looking at case studies, examples or problems. To lighten cognitive load, keep things simple and well organized. For example, devise an hour's lesson around four fifteen-minute chunks, each with an opportunity to create a simple mind map that summarizes the points learnt. Spend lots of time drilling and reviewing—the more you keep thinking about a particular point, the more chance it has of getting encoded into long-term memory.

Finally, get your student involved in these lesson plans or deliberations—explain how you're organizing concepts and mapping out ideas. Let them see the relationship between each of the concepts they're learning, and how it all fits together. Remember, the brain loves connections: the more *meaningful* connections you can draw between chunks of information, the better the brain will be able to file and retrieve that information later.

Scaffolding: the Power of Baby Steps

Being a good teacher is all about understanding how people naturally absorb, retain and use new information. If you think about any skill or knowledge you currently have, chances are you learnt it gradually, one step at a time. Experts always start out as novices, and the path from one to the other is filled with incremental changes rather than giant leaps.

The fancy name for this process of ramping up mastery from lower levels of capacity is called scaffolding, since it refers to the careful building of a complex mental structure with smaller, simpler units. The great thing about learning how to use scaffolding, as either a teacher or a student, is that it's a truly transferable skill—it's hard to imagine any domain in life where it isn't applicable.

Your overall goal as a teacher using the technique of scaffolding is to simplify. As we've seen, this reduces cognitive load because all the brain has to manage in working memory is a small chunk of information. Once this is banked in long-term memory, the next step, level or unit can be considered.

Depending on your student and what you're attempting to teach them, your scaffolding process can vary in complexity. For example, you might follow a series of graded stages to teach them how to use a piece of software they're unfamiliar with. Building a scaffold is like providing mental support and structure as the person builds up to the bigger goal: understanding how to use the entire program effectively.

You might start with *provision of knowledge*: you could give some explanations and instructions for the program, what it's used for, and a general introduction to the basic principles.

You could then move on to a *demonstration of strategies*: you might run through a few operations on the program, showing students exactly what to do to achieve certain outcomes, as they watch you.

You could extend this to *modeling*: this is where you construct a model encompassing the information you've shared, or show how the previous strategies fit together.

Next you could move to *questioning*: you might ask them to guess how to do another related operation, given what you've already shown them. Your demonstration might naturally prompt a question—what do we do if we want to perform a slightly different operation? Can we still use the same technique? This could be your cue to move on to showing them another, more complex strategy—providing they thoroughly understand the first one.

You could constantly make use of *instructing* as you go: tell your student, "you click here to do XYZ" or "this is how you import a file."

Throughout, you can offer *feedback and correction*: Ask a question, see how your student responds, and infer where their level of understanding is. Gently and positively offer corrections, backtracking to previous instructions or simpler concepts to check understanding. You might use general feedback like, "It's quicker to use a keyboard shortcut for that" or "you might want to try a different setting there."

Finally, you can make use of *restructuring the task* as you go: set your student mini-tasks to complete before tackling something more complicated, or deliberately ignore some aspects of the program you're teaching so you can make a particular point more clearly. You might show them how *not* to do something just so they understand why it doesn't work. For example, deliberately use the program incorrectly and let them see how it becomes unusable or crashes.

If all these steps sound complicated, they don't have to be—scaffolding can be subtle and spontaneous without losing its effectiveness. It might be as simple as reminding a child to slow down, read through the sentence again and sound out difficult words if necessary. Encourage your student to look at the simplest chunks first, and once they've mastered those, draw their attention to the connections between them using questions, prompts and clues. The best teachers are able to help a student arrive at the next level of complexity on their own—the best "lesson plan" is where the students themselves are eager to move onto the next step!

Another way to think about scaffolding is to imagine that it's a gradual process of "handing over" to the student—you slowly progress from teacher-centered to student-centered. This approach has been called "I do, we do, you do" or sometimes "show me, help me, let me." Let's look at each of the three steps using a simple example of teaching someone how to bake a tricky French souffle.

Teacher-led instruction, or "I do"

You tell your student to watch you carefully as you prepare the recipe, so they can see how it's done. As you do so, you give some instruction and direction, actively sharing knowledge which they passively receive. You want to cover all the new concepts, skills and information, for example, "I'm using a metal bowl, see? Metal bowls get squeaky clean and you don't want even the tiniest residue of any oil in there, or it will spoil your egg whites and they won't get to this stiff-peak stage."

At this stage, you are making sure your student is oriented to new material, and knows what the purpose of the lesson is (in this case, watch closely so you can do the same!). You want to clearly set limitations and goals, i.e. today we are making a perfect souffle. Draw on any previous knowledge, give meaningful and relevant explanations, and even examples.

Teacher and student cooperation, or "we do"

This is the part where you use "training wheels" and gradually ramp up your student's participation. You are still giving instruction, but it's now directed toward guiding their action. You could supervise them making a souffle using what you've taught them, although you're still there, doing some of the work, and prompting and correcting as you go. It's about providing an opportunity to practice a new skill or retrieve some stored information, but with a little support—psychological and cognitive.

Go one step at a time (remembering that sequences typically lower cognitive load) and use questions and prompts to lead the student to the next step. "OK, so now it's time to put it in the oven... Do you remember where in the oven it goes and why?" Encourage your student to demonstrate their understanding or skill in a limited way at first—a little encouragement and positive feedback is always appreciated! Mistakes are a part of the process, and will allow you to stop, adjust and reinforce the correct way.

Student-led practice, or "you do"

The ultimate goal is for your student to be able to perform the skill or retrieve the information on their own, without you. At some point, the training wheels come off. After some time you might ask your student to prepare a perfect souffle for you from scratch, without your supervision. This gives them the chance to independently demonstrate their progress, and compare this against the goals you both set in the beginning. Obviously, if your student produces what looks like a deflated hockey puck that was recently on fire, it's time to go back to the drawing board and build better scaffolding!

Takeaways

- We can draw on the five most common pedagogical approaches to become better teachers, whether that's inside the classroom or in more informal contexts.
- The constructivist approach is about building up knowledge and skill from

information that is already known to the student. You help them "construct" new knowledge by relating everything to this set of existing knowledge in order to connect two different concepts.

- The integrative approach focuses on making lessons practical and applicable in the real world. The more relevant and contextual new information is, the more likely students are to retain it.

- The collaborative approach uses the strengths of group collaboration between students to support learning. You rely on students within the group to teach each other by exposing them to unique viewpoints and knowledge that everyone has.

- The inquiry-based approach is about directing learning by asking the student to devise a question, a method for arriving at an answer, the answer, or some combination of these three.

- The reflective approach is about tailoring the teaching methods used to best fit the student in front of you, regularly taking time to appraise what works and what doesn't.

- The brain is not a machine. Cognitive load theory tells us that as the brain's power is limited, we need to think strategically and reduce load while maximizing learning. This can be done in a variety of ways that respect rather than push against the brain's natural learning processes. Some strategies involve keeping your material focused on particular topics, repeating information as much as you can, and appealing to the senses in ways that pique attention.

- Scaffolding is the principle of making small, incremental improvements and building bigger concepts or skills from smaller, simpler ones. This can be summarized as "I do, we do, you do" to show how the teacher gradually hands over control and mastery to the student.

Chapter 2. Seeing the Landscape

In all this talk of scaffolding, of laying out plans to reach goals, and of carefully organizing learning so that information is delivered in manageable chunks, you might have wondered: who gets to decide on these goals, these baby steps or these chunks? In the previous chapter we saw that it was important to lay out new information systematically for your student (after all, this is exactly what a teacher's job is) but then the question becomes, what's the best way to do this?

Good teachers have an advantage of perspective. Compared to their students, who can only see small and unclear sections of the bigger whole, the teacher can see it all, and understands how everything connects to the bigger picture. In fact it's this advantage in perspective that allows the teacher to impart anything of value to the student at all—otherwise, it would simply be two students blundering around together trying to find their way.

Good teachers can see the full "landscape" and know what's in front of them. This allows them to prioritize tasks, to frame things correctly, to set goals. This may seem unimportant if you're unused to teaching, but it is in fact the single most significant thing you do as a teacher, because it influences the entire way you think about the material in front of you, and how you convey it to your student.

Seeing the landscape incompletely or incorrectly means you give your student a faulty vision to work within, thus compromising their learning. Without a sensible road map through the territory, so to speak, you may get lost, find yourself disorganized or confused, or unable to anticipate or predict issues or opportunities ahead of you. On a more basic level, you simply won't inspire confidence or trust in the person you're trying to teach, and worse, you may teach them something entirely wrong.

If you think that being an expert in a certain field qualifies you to teach, since you are already familiar with the "map," think again. Teachers possess knowledge, but their main skill is in their conveying or communication of that knowledge. In a way, being a good teacher is not just about knowing the intellectual terrain, but also about knowing how to selectively ignore what isn't relevant in that terrain, so the student can focus on what is. If this weren't the case, people would be able to learn anything and everything perfectly using nothing more than Google or journal articles (hint: they can't!).

The teacher essentially constructs a truncated, simplified vision of the landscape—i.e. a map. This map is deliberately organized, abstracted and designed to make certain concepts understandable. It contains only those parts of your field of knowledge that are relevant for your student, right now, at their stage of learning and development. Yes, a map is simplified, but it should still be an accurate representation of the landscape. Though some detail may be omitted, the student shouldn't discover later that whole sections are just plain wrong.

It's worth dwelling on this map versus territory idea simply because so much misunderstanding and confusion can be avoided when a teacher approaches their task methodically and clearly. A proven study technique is to practice "teaching" the new material to someone else or give a little speech or presentation about the material you've just read. Similarly, many people say that if you cannot explain a project or idea to a non-expert or even a ten-year-old, then you don't *really* understand the concepts yourself, no matter how much of an expert you are.

Nothing will reveal gaps in your own knowledge like trying to teach someone else! Or rather, trying to teach will show you whether you are yourself working from inconsistent or incomplete maps or models. As a teacher, it's simply nonnegotiable: you cannot guide a novice through uncharted territory if you yourself are unclear of the lay of the land. The best teachers plot a course through a complex and new landscape before they set off, and they know where the final destination is even when the student doesn't.

How do we build good maps for our students? A map (or mental model) can be thought of as a series of *connections*. When we can put isolated ideas, concepts, events or theories into a bigger picture and link them together, we start to possess a broader, more organized and more coherent vision. We can make connections in time, by linking up what we learn now with what we've already learnt in the past, or we can make connections linking all the separate pieces of information we have to one another, in the present.

Connecting Old Knowledge to New

The wonderful thing about teaching is that you're never really starting "from scratch." Everybody has at least some pre-existing knowledge that you can build on—and that includes you as the teacher. Connecting old knowledge to new serves two functions: it allows people to understand and retain new information better, but it also gives you the chance as teacher to assess exactly where your student is, and if there are any gaps in their current understanding.

A physical map is only useful to you if you know where you are currently positioned on it, and in the same way you can't devise a route for your student unless you know the position they're starting from. A natural way to determine this is through simple questions to gauge your student's knowledge. What do they already know and understand? How do *they* envision their path and their ultimate goal? What do they consider their most important need and why?

Let's imagine an example where you are trying to help your younger brother with physics schoolwork. Before you can do anything, you need to understand where your bother is. If you can do this systematically, you will at the same time construct a loose lesson plan going forward. For example, you could get a piece of paper and literally sketch out a mind map of the material your brother is struggling with.

In the center of the mind map you might write "chapter 9" or "magnetism" and then draw branches off to indicate the different aspects of this topic that need to be understood and integrated. If possible, draw links between topics to indicate that they are connected. Once you've sketched out a loose mind map, you can start to see any gaps. You might ask your brother to rate the most difficult and challenging aspect, as well as tell you which parts are relatively easier, and which parts he understands well.

Just by doing this, you are already starting to illuminate a path for yourself. Can you *draw a path from what is known to what is unknown*, and see a way to take small steps from one to the other? You might notice that certain concepts from the earlier chapter on electricity are completely missing, and it's this lack of understanding that is making it hard for your student to grasp certain aspects of the current topic.

Many people don't bother with mind maps because they seem simple and pointless. But their simplicity is their strength. Sometimes, you really can't see a connection or link until you've literally put it down on paper. Don't just include what needs to be learnt on the map, but also include what is already learnt. Not only does this help you see what needs to be strengthened and reinforced, but it allows you to start organizing your plan to do so.

In quizzing your brother briefly, and hearing his appraisal on what's difficult, you start to understand that some of his difficulty in grasping magnetism is his incomplete knowledge of electrical charge, which itself is due to not properly understanding atomic structure, i.e. the relationship between an atom's electrons and its overall charge.

Knowing this, you have a road map planned out: start by reinforcing understanding of atomic structure, move to electrical charge, then tackle the issues he has with magnetism one by one, starting with those he already understands a little, then gradually moving to the most challenging.

This map helps both of you: he gets to work his way through the problems in a more manageable way, and you get to organize yourself and stay focused enough to keep guiding him toward the end destination. It's great for both teacher and student to see that the piece of knowledge or skill they're tackling is finite in size, and exactly where it fits into the bigger scheme of things. Students can often give up for exactly this reason: they don't know what they don't know, and they can't meaningfully connect any single exercise or explanation to the bigger picture, so it feels pointless.

Throughout this process, old knowledge is used to support and guide new knowledge. Always start by asking, "what do we already know?" and feel your way from there. Once you're aware of what your students already know— mind maps are one of many ways to help you with this—you can use their pre-existing knowledge to teach them in many effective ways. One such way is to problematize what your students already believe. When done right, this is easily the best way to gain attention, foster curiosity, and motivate students to learn more about something that they've discovered they don't know nearly as well as they thought they did.

Here's what this looks like in practice. Imagine you're teaching a course on nations and nationalism. On the first day, you ask your students to submit short writeups of what they think a nation is. For the next class, you take some of the most common responses and ask some of the students who gave them to elaborate on their thoughts. Then, you point out the problem with their explanation. This does not mean telling them they're wrong, but only that you need to expose the gaps in their knowledge.

For example, a student might say that a nation is just a group of people living somewhere. Ask them if they could settle somewhere with a couple of friends and call that area a nation. Another student might say that it's a collective of people with the same ethnicity. You can point out that many nations have various ethnicities in roughly the same proportion. Notice that you aren't saying that either of these two definitions is wrong. They're actually true in that nations do consist of people living together in a certain space, usually having the same ethnicity. But by showing that these definitions are incomplete, you nudge students to clarify their pre-existing knowledge and add to it in nuanced ways.

The Feynman technique

The ability to ask yourself questions as you learn, and as you move from known to unknown, is a key part of metacognition, or thinking about thinking. "Elaborative interrogation" is just one method of asking yourself questions that focuses on you seeing the whole picture behind a piece of information.

The Feynman Technique, named for famous physicist Richard Feynman, is another way of discussing with yourself. The Feynman Technique is a mental model that was coined by Nobel-prize-winning physicist Richard Feynman. Known as the "Great Explainer," Feynman was revered for his ability to clearly illustrate dense topics like quantum physics for virtually anybody. In "Feynman's Lost Lecture: The Motion of Planets Around the Sun," David Goodstein writes that Feynman prided himself on being able to explain the most complex ideas in the simplest terms. It stemmed from his own study techniques as a student at Princeton

University, and he refined the method as a professor and teacher of physics.

This method also allows you to gauge your comprehension of a given subject. Properly carried out, the Feynman technique will prove whether you really understand a topic or have glossed over certain important concepts. It's also suitable for almost every conceivable subject, allowing you to see the gaps in your knowledge that need to be corrected.

It's even simpler than the "why chain" utilized by children.

The Feynman technique helps to see what you are *unable* to answer—that is the information it provides. All you need to do is honestly answer the questions you are asking yourself, and you will quickly identify where you need to focus your attention. It has four steps.

Step One: Choose your concept.

The Feynman technique is widely applicable, so let's choose a concept we can use throughout this section: *gravity*. Suppose that we want to either understand the basics about gravity or explain it to someone else. Or, we want to see what level of understanding we have about gravity.

Step Two: Write down an explanation of the concept in plain English.

Can you do it? The simpler and shorter the explanation, the harder this is to do. This is the truly important step because it will show exactly what you do and do not understand about the concept of gravity. If you can boil information or a topic down to two sentences in a way that a five-year-old would understand, you probably have a level of mastery over it. If not, you've just found a chink in your armor.

So going back to the concept we are using, how would you define gravity? Would it be something about being attracted to large masses? Would it be something that makes us fall? Or would it be about how our planet was formed? Can you do it, or will you resort to saying, "Well, you know ... it's gravity!"

You might be able to explain what happens to objects that are subject to gravity *and* what happens when there is zero gravity. You might also be able to explain the causes of gravity. But everything that happens in between might be something you assume you know but continually skip learning about.

Where does your explanation start to fall apart? If you can't perform this step, clearly you don't know as much about it as you thought, and you would be terrible at explaining it to someone else. The same goes if your explanations are long, rambling, and deflective. Coincidentally, this is why teaching a skill or information to others is such a powerful tool for your own learning. It forces you to re-examine what you know, and package it all in a way that allows someone else to have a complete understanding as well.

Step Three: Find your blind spots.

If you were unable to come up with a short description of gravity in the previous step, then it's clear you have large gaps in your knowledge. This step implores you to research gravity and learn enough to be able to describe it in a simple way. You might come up with something like, "The force that causes larger objects to attract smaller objects because of their weight and mass." Whatever you are unable to explain, this is a blind spot you must rectify.

Being able to analyze information and break it down in a simple way demonstrates knowledge and understanding. If you can't summarize it in one sentence, or at least in a brief and concise manner, you still have blind spots you need to learn about. This is a non-negotiable aspect of the technique.

I encourage you to take a second and try this right now. What seemingly simple concept can you try to explain? Can you actually do it, or does it reveal a lack of understanding somewhere in the process?

For instance, why is the sky blue? How do television remotes work? How does lightning appear? What are clouds made out of? What is digestion? These might be questions you can answer on a surface level, but then what?

Step Four: Use an analogy.

Finally, create an analogy for the concept. What is the purpose of this step? It's an extension of step three. Making analogies between concepts requires a deep understanding of the main traits and characteristics of each, and you can even transfer that understanding into different contexts. You can look at it as the true test of your understanding and whether you still possess blind spots in your knowledge.

What would an analogy for gravity be? Gravity is like when you put your foot into a puddle, and the leaves on the surface of the water are attracted to it because of an invisible attraction to the mass of your foot. That attraction is gravity.

This step also connects new information to old information and lets you piggyback off a working mental model to understand or explain in greater depth. Of course, it's unlikely that you can do step four if you can't do step two and three, but sometimes you can complete steps two and three and find you can't master step four. Now you understand the boundaries of your knowledge.

The Feynman technique is a rapid way to discover what you know versus what you think you know, and it allows you to solidify your knowledge base. When you keep explaining and simplifying to yourself and discover that you can't, you've just discovered that you don't know as much as you thought you did.

Generating a Concept Map

There's no need to get too caught up in drawing a literal "mind map" when trying to understand your cognitive blind spots. The way you

49

visually and conceptually organize the material will naturally depend on the topic at hand, and a mind map might not always be the best fit. But it's almost certain that your topic can be broken down into smaller and simpler subunits that connect meaningfully to one another.

Can you think of any categories or even steps in a sequence to help you lay out the information in a more organized way? Can you see the topic through different lenses or according to different layers or models? What are the simple concepts that need to be in place to grasp the bigger, more complex idea?

If you were teaching photosynthesis, for example, you could note that to understand the process you'd need both a good understanding of the chemical processes involved, but also the physiological structures inside the cell where these processes take place. Finally, you'd need a way to join these two different aspects together. Your map or outline might include a table showing clearly which process occurs, in what order, and in what exact part of the cell. Not only does this organize your efforts, but you'll be left with a useful summary for your student to study from at the end.

If you were teaching someone how to construct a wedding bouquet from scratch, however, your approach would obviously be different. Just because some skills and knowledge are not what we normally think of as academic, it doesn't mean they can't benefit from pen, paper and a methodical approach. You could sit with your student and together construct a loose mind map, outlining first your general aim, and then breaking elements down into a logical sequence that builds. Start by outlining the "skeleton" of the bouquet, then fill in with contrasting foliage types, then add smaller supporting flowers in a zigzag pattern, then introduce accent flowers, and so on.

What's important is that your map is clearly showing *connections*, or relationships between different subunits. This is what allows your student to pull everything together into a unified whole. There are no standard formulas or rules for effective "maps" when it comes to teaching, since the possibilities for what can be taught are endless, each quite unique. However, ask yourself the following the next time you're preparing to teach someone and want to be thorough and methodical:

- Have you broken down the new information into genuinely manageable small chunks? Or could you separate it further?
- Have you shown the connections and relationships between these chunks? For example, have you illustrated the hierarchy between them?
- Are you being as clear and simple as possible?
- Does your map actually go somewhere specific, i.e. do you have a fixed endpoint in mind?
- Can you see how each of the subunits relates to this end point?
- Are there any gaps in the plan, in other words, have you made any assumptions about what your student already knows?
- Have you included what your student already knows, and are you drawing links between that and the material they don't yet understand?

If you ask the student to generate this kind of map themselves, they not only hone in on the areas they need to focus on, but they give you some direction when it comes to quizzing or testing them. It can be a learning experience in itself to try to construct the map, and you can begin teaching while correcting and fine tuning the map. After all, many students have trouble not with the material per se, but the *way* in which their isolated pieces of information fit together as a whole.

A concept map is invaluable. You could use it to have the student make and test their own hypothesis, or make predictions, i.e. the map can help them structure and direct their inquiry going forward. The map serves to solidify understanding and strengthen skills. If the topic is not a practical one, your student can still conduct thought experiments or ask hypothetical questions—you'll recognize this as a variation of the inquiry-based approach, where the student uses the map to generate their own question, their own answer, and their own means of getting to that answer.

For example, you could be teaching someone about how to solder. One part of your map could include details on what solder is actually made of, and why. Looking at this, the student could make a prediction: altering the composition of solder could change its melting point, which would affect how it could be used. They could test this themselves and see what happens, and if it keeps happening on different base materials. In doing so, the student is actually teaching themselves about the relationship between composition, melting point and solder properties.

This is why integrated or contextual learning is often so effective—because it allows us to quickly and easily establish meaningful connections between loose pieces of information. We don't just *know* something, we *understand* it, from the inside out. The next time such a student is faced with a poor solder, for example, he can more accurately diagnose the problem or even predict its composition based on its appearance. In essence, he has internalized his own mental map and can use this himself to navigate the topic, without a teacher. This brings us neatly to another important aspect of creating links that help understanding: the ability to make analogies.

Make the Most of Analogies

Aside from using different types of analogies to improve your retention of learning materials, there are some science-backed tips you can employ to further enhance how productive these analogies can be for your studies. These are:

1) Use multiple analogies for the same topic

This one goes without saying, but using different types of analogies in your learning will ensure that you've grasped your content beyond just a superficial understanding. Since analogies force you to make transfers mentally, they challenge your comprehension of key concepts in different ways depending on the type you use. Generally, it's a good idea to use as many as you can that seem relevant to your topic.

For example, let's say you're learning about the theory of liberalism. The first type of analogy you can use is Antonym. If we think of hot and cold as opposites, what would be a similar antonym for liberalism? This could be either communism or conservatism. Next, we can utilize Example/Type Of analogies. Liberalism is a type of political ideology, in the same way that iPhones are a type of smartphone.

A third type of analogy we can attempt is Thing/Characteristic. What is a characteristic of liberalism similar to auditory volume as a characteristic of speakers? One answer is human rights. Likewise, you can utilize multiple analogies for your own concepts and topics.

2) Use examples to constantly reaffirm your learning

This insight has been derived from the studies of Daniel Schwartz and John Bransford. The usage of examples is important because it helps novices and beginners learn through their own knowledge of the content of those examples. Experts can skip examples because they are already intimately aware of the subject matter. But in most instances, examples help you make sense of complex ideas and provide yourself with tools to remember them more efficiently.

If you're studying ethical systems, make a note of different situations in which they apply. Should you lie to your friend when you don't want to talk to them by saying you're busy? Why or why not? If you have to divide a pie between three people, what would be the fairest way to cut it? Examples like these liven up your studying, as they make dry content much more realistic and relevant to the world around you.

3) Remember the purpose of the analogy

Oftentimes it is easy to use analogies to understand particular concepts mechanically, yet forget why the analogy is appropriate in the first place. For example, if a student is asked what mitochondria is, they say "it is the powerhouse of the cell" since that is a standard analogy across biology textbooks. However, many remember the comparison without understanding what it means for mitochondria to be the powerhouse of a cell.

One way to avoid this issue is to frame your analogies in ways that clearly indicate the purpose or role of the comparison. In the case of mitochondria, consider what function it would have to fulfill to be a "powerhouse" for the cell. It would have to provide the cell with power, which is more accurately referred to as energy.

Another thing you can do is to list a few drawbacks of the analogy. "Powerhouse" can imply that it merely stores energy, but in fact mitochondria is responsible for the extracting, processing, and releasing of energy to cells. It isn't enough to simply remember the analogy; you must know why it is an appropriate one to use as well, and these are a few ways to do just that.

4) Reserve analogies for more difficult concepts

While it may be tempting to use analogies throughout your studies, it is advisable to reserve their usage for more complex ideas.

Students often find that utilizing analogies for easier concepts and information can cause mental confusion and clutter.

When something is easily understandable, you don't need to break it down further for better retention. Focus your energy on more difficult concepts, especially since you'll be using multiple analogies for the same concept.

Make a list of all the ones you use, list some drawbacks for each, and use visual cues if possible. Employing both visual and text-based cues is a good way to improve retention and understanding according to multimedia learning theory. Also use appropriate comparisons for your analogy on the left-hand side of the academic analogy format. This will make the relation between the main components of your analogy clearer without requiring too much re-reading.

Analogy Thinking

Let's dive a bit deeper into a specific type of analogy thinking.

How might you explain a new business to someone who is clueless in the space? "It's like the Uber of X, except A, B, and C."

When we seek to make ourselves understand an idea, we often default to analogies. They provide instant understanding and context, because our thoughts are able to focus on a singular concept and then slowly start to differentiate to the point of comprehension.

And of course, linking new concepts and information through analogy is another great method to cement learning into the knowledge pool. Despite our natural tendencies, analogies are underrated and overlooked as important parts of human cognition. In contrast to this presumption, some neuroscientists, such as Indiana University Professor Douglas Hofstadter, assert that analogies are the foundation of all human thought.

His reasoning is that analogies allow us to understand categories, and categories are how we distinguish information and concepts from each other. It's our ability to identify likenesses—a form of analogy-making—that allows us to discern similarities and thus categorize objects in different ways.

This is easy to see if you consider how we categorize animals. To an untrained eye, a dog and a cat might seem distinctly similar. They both have fur, four legs, and a tail, but their different faces, diets, behavior, and evolutionary heritage allow us to differentiate between the two of them. They are comparable animals, analogous to each other, but they are more closely analogous to their own species, and that is what allows us to place them in their respective categories of dog or cat. But all that means is that we would never use dogs to describe cats, or vice versa.

Even more complex, higher-order ideas are formed by making analogies. Consider the more abstract group of mammal. This group compares dogs to cats while counting them as similar, but also includes animals as diverse as the platypus, dolphin, and opossum. No one would look at a dolphin and believe it was similar to a housecat, but the science is very clear. Lactating, having hair or fur, and being warm-blooded are the only criteria that must be met to put creatures into the group of mammal. If they share those characteristics, they are mammals.

Grouping those criteria together allows us to form the higher-order idea of mammal, which enables us to discern which creatures fit the bill. This group of criteria that we simplify into the word *mammal* is what allows us to see dolphins and platypuses as analogous to each other.

Our understanding, and thus the analogies we use to describe the world, evolve as we age and are exposed to ideas in our lives and our cultures. But no matter what we learn, it must be filtered through a brain that categorizes, and thus understands, the world by forming analogies and discerning differences between objects and ideas. When we consciously distinguish different elements and create analogies while learning new information, we speed up the process of integrating our new knowledge into our minds.

Now that we've covered the overall cognitive role and importance of analogy, how can we use it to self-learn and understand more effectively? As we mentioned, analogies provide instant context—a mental model for the information you are looking at—and then you are left to slowly differentiate and flesh out the details.

For instance, earlier we mentioned that new businesses are frequently described as "the Uber of X." Uber is a rideshare company that functions by calling non-taxi drivers to help transport you using their own personal cars.

Thus, anything described as "the Uber of X" would be implied to involve people with their own cars, delivering or driving people or things. Okay, we've got a mental image now—a good idea of what's involved, what the purpose is, and how it functions.

Now the important bit of learning comes—how do you differentiate this new business from Uber itself? What nuanced factors make it something other than a clone of Uber? Well, this element, as well as what you are comparing the new business to, is up to you to articulate. When you take a new piece of information and intentionally find a way to create an analogy with it, you are (1) finding a similar model of information that requires understanding enough to compare and contrast two concepts, and (2) further understanding the two models well enough to state how they differ. That's where the deeper learning synthesis occurs.

For instance, what if you wanted to create an analogy around learning the steps involved in creating a new piece of legislation? Abide by the two steps above. You would first find an existing, familiar piece of information that the process for new legislation reminds you of. Search your memory banks for something similar; this type of analysis of major and minor factors is helpful to your learning.

Next, how do they differ? This is where you can clearly demonstrate the difference between concepts, based on a deep understanding. Pick out small details and note how they appear similar but come from totally different motivations. Document what this all means for new legislation.

This is far more than a thought exercise of comparing two different concepts—it's combining old information with new and forcing them to interact toward greater comprehension and memorization.

Takeaways

- Excellent teachers know how to "see the landscape" ahead of them, and their understanding of the field of learning allows them to set goals and parameters, prioritize and frame tasks, and gauge their students' current understanding.
- Concept maps are simplified models of more complex material that make clear the connections between different ideas. Concept maps can be drawn by both student and teacher to gauge knowledge

gaps, plan lessons, learn those lessons, and assess the effectiveness of that learning.

- Concept maps consist of simplified chunks or pieces of information arranged to highlight the relationships or connections between them. A good concept map is relevant, simple, accurate and draws on existing mental models and knowledge.

- Once you've identified what your student already knows, the next step is planning how to utilize that. In some cases, this will be easy in that you only need to teach them certain concepts that will help them understand the topic you wanted to teach them in the first place. However, you could also combine the usage of concept-based maps with an inquiry-based approach and problematize what students already know in order to make them curious and eager to learn more.

- The Feynman technique is a "bigger picture" technique that allows both teacher and student to identify their own mental blind spots. First, identify the concept in question, then write down an explanation of it in plain English, then identify any areas where the explanation fails or where data is missing. Then, use the power of analogy to fill in the gaps, i.e. use pre-existing mental models to better understand new material.

- Analogies can aid learning because they connect old knowledge with new. Analogies can be Antonyms, Types, or Characteristics, each expressing the qualities of a new concept in terms of already understood concepts. Analogies are best when as many are used as possible, and they encourage higher-order abstract thinking.

Chapter 3. The Nuts and Bolts

The previous chapters have covered basic principles and theoretical approaches to adopt as you set out on the task of becoming the best teacher you can. But you might have read all this and wondered what it actually looked like, in practice. In this chapter, we're digging into the more hands-on aspects of teaching, and looking at a few popular methods and techniques for applying the philosophy we've already outlined. So, as you read, bear in mind that the technique is much the same, whether you're a teacher, a student, or a bit of both.

You are essentially looking at the same process from two different sides—teacher and student; the more you understand about these two different perspectives, the more enriched you'll be, whether you're trying to learn about XYZ or help someone else learn about it. In fact, this is the reason that many teacher training programs have trainee teachers deliberately take on the role of student as an exercise, so they can better understand the "other side" and more effectively cross the divide. Now, let's dive in.

The SQ3R Method

For the large majority of school subjects, textbooks are the core of the study program along with lectures and discussions. A typical teacher's entire lesson plan for a year usually draws from the structure and sequence of at least one textbook. These volumes are, more often than not, forbiddingly big. Multiply one large book by the number of classes a student has in any given semester and you've got a seriously overweight backpack—nearly as heavy as every one of your teachers' expectations that you read every single one.

Textbooks are dense, detailed, heavily annotated, and long. It's easy to conjure up the image of a student late at night, glossing over page 349 of a giant volume, growing fatigued and unable to retain the words they're reading the next morning.

That's why American educator Francis P. Robinson developed a method meant to help students really get the most comprehension from the texts they're assigned—and, ergo, the subject they're studying. Robinson sought a way to make reading more active, helping readers by creating dynamic engagement with books so the information stuck in their minds.

The traditional classroom setting of reading and regurgitating certainly isn't the most effective, but it's the only model most of us know. Robinson's more engaging approach is suitable for more than just reading: your entire study plan can be modeled on Robinson's method and adapted to your self-learning.

The technique is called The SQ3R method, named for its five components:

- survey

- question

- read

- recite

- review

Survey. The first step in the method is getting a general overview of what you'll be reading. Textbooks and nonfiction works aren't like fiction or narrative literature in which you just start from the beginning and wind your way through each chapter. The best works of nonfiction are arranged to impart information in a way that's clear and memorable and builds upon each previous chapter. If you dive in without surveying first, you are going in blind, without understanding where you're heading and what you're trying to accomplish. You should get a lay of the land first, *before* you delve into Chapter 1. The survey component allows you to get the most general introduction to the topic so you can establish and shape the goals you want to achieve from reading the book.

It's just like taking a look at the entire map before you set off on a road trip. You may not need all the knowledge at the moment, but understanding everything as a whole and how it fits together will help you with the small details and when you're in the weeds. You'll know that you generally need to head southwest if you're confused.

In the SQ3R method, surveying means examining the structure of the work: the book title, the introduction or preface, section titles, chapter titles, headings and subheadings. If the book is illustrated with pictures or graphics, you'd review them. You could also make note of the conventions the book uses to guide your reading: typefaces, bold or italic text, and chapter objectives and study questions if they're in there. In using the survey step, you're setting up expectations for what you're going to be reading about and giving yourself an initial framework to structure your goals for reading the material.

For example, let's say you're reading a book to learn more about geology. I happen to have one called *Geology Illustrated* by John S. Shelton— it's about fifty years old and no longer in print, but it works fine for our purposes.

There's a preface describing what's in the book and how the illustrations are arranged. There's an unusually extensive table of contents, divided into parts: "Materials," "Structure," "Sculpture," "Time," "Case Histories," and "Implications." That tells me that the book will start with concrete (excuse the pun) geological elements, will flow into how they form over time, important incidents, and what we might expect in the future. That's a pretty good guess at the arc of the book.

Each part is then divided into chapters, which are further divided into a ton of headings and subheadings—too many to mention here, but they give a more nuanced summary of what each part will go into. When you survey and know the significance of what you're currently learning, you are able to instantly comprehend it better. It's the difference between looking at a single gear in isolation versus seeing where and how it works in a complex clock.

Beyond books, you should survey all the important concepts in a discipline. If you can't find it within a structure like a book's table of contents, then you need to be able to create it for yourself. Yes, this is the difficult part, but once you are able to lay all the concepts out and understand how they relate to each other at least on a surface level, you will already be leaps ahead of others. Use the survey component to form an outline of what you'll learn. In a sense, it's more like you're plotting out a metaphorical "book" for yourself.

You want to form a general outline of what you're going to learn. Since you're studying this on your own, there might be a few gaps in what you think you'll need to know. So in this phase, you'll determine exactly what you *want* to become knowledgeable about, as specifically as you can. For example, if you want to learn all about psychology, that's going to take a significant amount of time. It won't happen in one shot. You'd want to specify it a little more: the early history of psychoanalysis, the works of Sigmund Freud and Carl Jung, sports psychology, developmental psychology—the possibilities are plenty.

You'll want to keep an eye out for phrases or concepts that appear in several different sources, since they represent elements that come up often in your chosen field and might be things you have to know. Draw connections and cause-and-effect relationships before even diving into any of the concepts in detail.

For example, let's say you want to study the history of European cinema. Entering "European cinema history" into Google brings up a lot of interesting possibilities, and some of those can be used to form the outline you want.

You can look for reading materials on Amazon.com, finding the ones that seem the most authoritative. The Internet Movie Database (IMDB) can help you find the most important European films for you to watch. You can discover which European directors are the most cited and appear to be the most important and influential. You can research which European movies are the highest rated and why. You can collect a few resources on what specific countries had what cinematic movements and why.

Then you'll organize these resources. You'll come up with a plan to study each one—perhaps study a chapter in a book on early European film history, then watch a couple of films that represent the era you're on at the moment and give yourself a film review assignment afterward. Focus on gathering and organizing; you don't need to touch these resources yet. The important aspect is that you've surveyed the topic before diving in and thus understand what you're getting into and why.

Question. In the second stage of the SQ3R method, you're still not diving into the deep end. During the question stage, you'll work a little more deeply to get your mind more prepared to focus and interact with the material you're reading. You'll take a slightly closer look at the structure of the book and form some questions you'd like to answer or set up the objectives you want to achieve.

In the question phase of reading a book—or, more precisely at this point, *preparing* to read—you'd go through the chapter titles, headings, and subheadings and rephrase them in the form of a question. This turns the dry title the author has given into a challenge or problem for you to solve. For example, if you're reading a book on Freud, there might be a chapter called "Foundations of Freud's Analyses of Dreams." You'd rewrite this chapter title as "How did Sigmund Freud's work on dream interpretation originate and what were his very first ideas on the subject?" You could pencil that question in the margin of your book. If you're reading a textbook with study questions at the ends of the chapters, those serve as excellent guides to what you're about to find out.

In the geology book, I'm afraid there aren't too many chapter titles that I could rephrase as inquiries. ("Weathering," "Groundwater," "Glaciation"—that's about it.) But there are headings that might work: "Some Effects of Metamorphism on Sedimentary Rocks," for example, can become "What can happen to bottom-centered rocks through eons of environmental change?" Not only have I changed it to a question, but I've paraphrased the title into wording that I can understand even before I've started reading.

Now that you've organized your resources for study planning, you can arrange some of the topics you're going to cover into questions you want answered or objectives that you want to meet. Based on the source material you've lined up and the patterns that you might have observed, what specific answers are you hoping to find in your studies? Write them down. This is also a good time to come up with a structure for answering your questions—a daily journal, a self-administered quiz, some kind of "knowledge tracker"? You don't have to answer the questions yet—you just need to know how you're going to record them when you do.

In our European film history example, if you've done even the most cursory investigation in the survey phase, you undoubtedly came across some directors' names more than once: Federico Fellini, Jean-Luc Godard, Luis Buñuel, Fritz Lang, and so forth. You figure they're going to be important people to get to know, so you could ask the question, "Why was Fellini so influential?" "What was Buñuel's directing style?" "What themes did Godard pursue in his filmmaking?" You might have come across certain concepts or themes that seemed common in European film—"French New Wave," "World War II," "neo-realism," for example. Put these down as targets for your study and arrange them into your outline.

Reading. In this stage you're finally ready to dive into the material. Because you've gotten the lay of the land and formed some questions and goals for your studies, you're a little more engaged when you finally sit down to read. You're looking for answers to the questions you've raised. Another underrated aspect of formulating and organizing before you actually begin reading is to build *anticipation* for learning. You've been looking over everything for a while now, and you'll probably be eager to finally dive in and answer the questions you've been mentally accumulating.

This step is where most people try to start but fail because they lack a foundation and instead have unreasonable expectations.

Now you're being deliberate and paced about your reading so you can comprehend better. This means slowing down—a *lot*. Be patient with the material and with yourself. If a passage is difficult to understand, read it extremely slowly. If you aren't getting a sense of clarity about a certain part, stop, go back to the beginning, and reread it. It's not like you're reading a page-turner novel that you can't put down. You're taking in information that might be densely packed—so read it slowly and attentively, one section at a time.

Chances are that reading is part of your study plan, but so might be visual aids, online courses, and Internet resources. Use them exactly the way you'd use the book in the reading phase: deliberately and persistently, with the goal of fully understanding each concept you're being taught. If you get lost, remember the rewind button and scrolling are your best buddies. Plan your study time around getting as complete a level of comprehensiveness as you can.

With our European film history example, this is obvious. Watch your films with a critical eye. At certain points you might want to rewind to catch visual images, dialogue, or action that might be pertinent. If you can watch a video with a director's commentary audio track, you'll want to spend an afternoon with that. Cross-check the movies with the books you're reading or the online courses you're taking to answer any questions or lines of thought that you might have.

Reciting. This step is crucial in processing the information you're learning and is the biggest difference between reading to learn and reading for entertainment. Now that you're familiar with the material, the aim of the reciting phase is to reorient your mind and attention to focus and learn more fully as you go along. In other words, this step is about literal recitation.

Ask questions—out loud, verbally—about what you're reading. This is also the point where you take copious notes in the margins of the text and underline or highlight key points. Recitation is verbal and also through writing. However, it's important to restate these points *in your own words* rather than just copy phrases from the book onto a piece of paper. By doing this, you're taking the new knowledge and putting it into phrases of which you already know the meaning. This makes the information easier to grasp in a language you understand. It makes it significant and meaningful to you.

My geology book happens to have pretty wide margins on the sides of the pages, so I have some nice room to rephrase and rewrite key points as well as highlight important concepts. For example, consider the following original text:

> "This comparison suggests that the slow progress of erosion on hills and mountains is similar to the much more rapid and observable changes seen in miniature all about us."

I could rewrite the above into something like this:

> "Mountains and hills experience the same decay as happens in lowlands and rivers, just more slowly. Similar to baseball players."

What I'm doing here is putting one single bit of information into two distinct phrases, one of which I had to come up with myself. This is a huge tool that's used in memorization, and it's also a great way to make the information more meaningful to me personally. I also added a bit about baseball because I like baseball, and it makes the concept instantly understandable when I look back at it. Repeated throughout the course of a whole book, this process multiplies your learning capacity by itself.

The recitation phase in organizing your studies is great because it works across different mediums, and there are plenty of ways you can express your questions and restatements.

Going back to our European cinema example, if you're watching Ingmar Bergman's *The Seventh Seal* (short summary: medieval knight meets angel of death, tries to buy time by playing chess with him), you might write down questions about its Biblical references, the art direction, the Middle Ages references, or the cinematography. You could also write a summary or do a video blog of the movie and address the key sequences that are most relevant to your questions. You could also compare it to other films by Bergman or note similarities his style has with other directors that you're studying. The important part is that you are taking the time to rephrase and recite new knowledge and make it meaningful to you—and no one else.

Review. The final stage of the SQ3R plan is when you go back over the material that you've studied, re-familiarize yourself with the most important points, and build your skills at memorizing the material.

Robinson breaks this stage down into specific days of the week, but we'll just mention some of the tactics in general. They include writing more questions about important parts you have highlighted, orally answering some of the questions if you can, reviewing your notes, creating flashcards for important concepts and terminology, rewriting the table of contents using your own words, and building out a mind map. Any kind of practice that helps you drill down, take in, and commit information to memory is fair game (though flashcards are especially effective).

This step is meant to strengthen your memory of the material, but it does more than that. It can help you see connections and similarities between different aspects that you might not have picked up at first and put concepts and ideas into greater context. It can also improve your mental organization skills so you can use this practice for other topics.

Think of this step as the natural continuation of the survey step. At this point, you've gained an outline of the field, you've gotten into the nitty-gritty, and now you should take a step back, reevaluate, and make updated, more accurate, and insightful connections. Pair that with memorization, and your path to self-learning and expertise becomes essentially a shortcut.

My geology book has no shortage of terms that I could put onto flashcards. "Monocline," "stratification," "glacial scour"—whip out the Sharpie now. But I could also map out the process of glaciation in a flowchart or some other visual medium. I could make a timeline of the ages of the earth and link it with the most significant geological changes that took place during each era. I can also take down questions that come up that the book either left unanswered or made me want to investigate more fully.

You can use most elements of the book review phase for study planning in the same way. In our European cinema example, you could make a catalog or database for European film directors that outlines their work, their main themes, or their stylistic choices. You can draw up flashcards that will help you recall the important facets of different European strains: "neo-realism," "giallo horror," "spaghetti Western," and "cinéma du look." And of course you can journal what you've learned, either in written form or some visual expression.

The SQ3R method is no joke. It's exhaustive and detailed and will take patience and sharp organization to pull off. But if you give yourself the patience and devotion to take each step seriously and slowly, you'll find it incredibly helpful to tackle a complex subject. And each time you do it, it's a little easier than the last.

In explaining the SQ3R method, we briefly skimmed the role of organization and notes and how they impact self-learning. After all, you can't organize everything in your head only and hope to be effective. When you eventually need to write down what you've learned or organized, there is a specific method of note-taking that will be most beneficial.

Abide by Bloom

Another useful tool is called Bloom's taxonomy, created by Benjamin Bloom in 1956 (though updated in 2001) as a way to measure the academic performance of college students. It has since been a staple in academic institutions as a framework for crafting lessons that ensure a thorough comprehension in students. For our purposes, it's a literal step-by-step guideline for what is necessary to move your understanding forward.

Bloom's taxonomy essentially states that for the highest level of subject understanding (i.e. expertise), there are six sequential levels we must be able to complete. Most people will never make it through all the levels in the taxonomy, so don't let yourself fall victim to that fate. The current taxonomy's levels are, from lowest to highest level of understanding, as follows:

- Remember. Retrieving, recognizing, and recalling relevant knowledge from long-term memory.
- Understand. Constructing meaning from oral, written, and graphic messages through interpreting, exemplifying, classifying, summarizing, inferring, comparing, and explaining.
- Apply. Carrying out or using a procedure for executing or implementing.
- Analyze. Breaking material into constituent parts and determining how the parts relate to one another and to an overall structure or purpose through differentiating, organizing, and attributing.

- Evaluate. Making judgments based on criteria and standards through checking and critiquing.
- Create. Putting elements together to form a coherent or functional whole; reorganizing elements into a new pattern or structure through generating, planning, or producing.

Once you hit the top level of "create," then you can be considered to have a deep grasp on a subject. Yet without advancing through each level of the taxonomy, you can't adequately perform the next levels. We see this illustrated in our lives every day when someone who doesn't have an adequate understanding of a topic seeks to evaluate it and make a judgment upon it. That's because of a failure to follow the taxonomy!

Bloom's taxonomy is a particularly useful tool to help guide and shape your learning process. Basically, the taxonomy is a list of *how* to actively build expertise in a subject matter. It focuses on the mental processes that allow you to frame information and analyze it, each verb a kind of mental tool to grasp and manipulate new incoming data. Bloom's framework is great because it's so versatile and can be used literally anywhere. In the classroom, at work, or in designing your own systems for achieving your personal goals, this taxonomy gives you a shorthand to work with.

The entire taxonomy is predicated on the mental process of learning, which can actually be summed up quite nicely. Before you can **understand** a concept, you must **remember** it. To **apply** a concept, you must first **understand** it. In order to **evaluate** a process, you must have **analyzed** it. To **create** an accurate conclusion, you must have completed a thorough **evaluation**. The challenge is introspection and understanding where you currently fall on the taxonomy, because only then can you pinpoint what is required for you to move forward in your mastery.

Let's dive into each element more deeply.

First, *remembering* contains elements like *listening*, *finding* information (using tools like *Googling*, perhaps), actively *memorizing* data, *bookmarking* important information to return to later, *highlighting* key points to synthesize later, and *repeating* information again and again to drill it.

This aspect is all about taking information and fixing it somehow so that you can store it and retrieve it later. If you're the kind of person who likes to make extensive bookmarks and notes about things you want to read or watch in the future, then you are actively remembering. You are also helping your long-term memory put down information whenever you tabulate or place information in easy-to-remember bullet points. Remembering also entails outlining key features or quotes or defining the main ideas so that you can recall the summary later on. Whenever you revise for an exam, you're using these skills.

Understanding happens whenever we engage with information more actively. Whereas remembering is about concretizing and storing information, understanding involves picking it all apart to better see how it works, like some people do to household appliances! *Categorizing* data (like we're doing here), *grouping* information into chunks, *inferring* from the data you have and *predicting* future events based on it, *summarizing*, and *paraphrasing* in different words are all cognitive operations intended to get to the deeper meaning of a set of symbols or patterns.

Teachers who ask their students to write things "in their own words" are doing so because they don't want to test for memorization; they want to test for understanding. If you comprehend a thing deeply, you are able to manipulate it, no matter how its components are rearranged or what symbols are used to express it. If you've ever tried to explain something complicated to someone who's not familiar with the concept, you may have found it helpful to give them a related example. You could outline a metaphor from a concept that they'd understand more easily and show how the ideas relate to one another. This *relating* and *associating* is key to developing deep understanding of a topic.

Applying is the third category. This is, broadly, where information is brought into the "real world" and made manifest, whether that's by *executing*, *sketching*, *acting out*, or *articulating*. As you're probably noticing, many of these terms have significant overlap with other verbs in other categories—and this should obviously be the case, when you consider that the brain isn't ever truly performing discrete activities, but rather flowing in one continuous action that, for our purposes, we're trying to understand using different models.

In fact, Bloom's verb taxonomy is itself a form of "applying"—it's *charting* or *presenting* information in a concrete way—i.e., applying the abstract concepts to make manifest a model, idea, or concept. *Painting*, *preparing*, *displaying*, *reenacting*, and even *playing* are all verbs associated with this category of the taxonomy. Every time you make a pie chart to illustrate data, turn a plan into reality, or design an experiment that actually gets carried out, you're "applying."

The fourth category is *analyzing*, which is pretty self-explanatory. Verbs in this category include *questioning*, *explaining*, *organizing*, *deconstructing*, *correlating*, and *calculating*. This includes all those verbs that show us actively operating on and manipulating information that comes in, not just to pass it from one form to another, but to look closely at its constituents, trying to understand them. Bloom's theory itself is an example of *appraising* and *categorizing*. You're participating in these functions when you draw a mind map, integrate one set of ideas with another set, break down a machine into its components, or ask, "Why is this happening?"

The fifth element is *evaluating*, and it includes any verbs that show we're applying some value judgments to the material in front of us. In the previous category, analysis is value-neutral and merely about understanding. This category, however, concerns things like *criticizing*, *rating*, *reflecting*, *reviewing*, *assessing*, and *validating*. This is where our brains practice discernment—and the weighing up of the information against stated goals. How useful are the results of your experiment? What is the quality and veracity of the claims you're appraising? How well did you perform? How can you *editorialize* or else compile all this information into a whole that actually says something?

The final verb group is *creating*. Here, our relationship to information is quite fundamental: we make it! *Composing* music, *mixing* known things to create something new, *filming* a movie, *writing* the script, and *role-playing* the characters are all creative ways to engage with information and build something novel. Other creative endeavors you might not have thought of include *programming*, *designing* systems, *adapting* material from one form into another, or even things like *podcasting* or *blogging*. Interestingly, Bloom even considered *leading* to be creative, since leadership often involves guiding people toward an entirely new and self-made vision.

Again, these verbs and categories will always overlap—the point is not to identify discrete categories. Rather, this model is a tool to help you play with information and see it from many different angles, in the same way as a toolbox of differently colored glasses could be worn to look at the same information in varying lights. When you're trying to learn and memorize, it makes a huge difference to engage actively and deliberately with information—not just in one or two ways, but in as many as possible. This way, data comes alive, becoming three-dimensional and allowing you a depth of understanding that will last longer than more shallow impressions.

Whenever you're learning something new, you might, for example, highlight the text in the book so you can summarize it (remembering) and then paraphrase that text in your own words (understanding). You can then apply your understanding by constructing your own chart or diagram (applying) and taking some time to break that diagram down, question it, and link it to other diagrams you've already made (analyzing). You can ask yourself after all this whether these methods are actually helping you retain the material (evaluating) and use your assessment to guide the further development of improved systems of learning (creating).

It sounds tedious, and it can be, but that's the true path to information synthesis. In fact, it's this tough mental work and struggle that really cements concepts and facts in your brain.

Spaced Repetition

The first method is directly aimed at dealing with beating forgetting. Spaced repetition— otherwise known as distributed practice—is just what it sounds like.

The reason it is such an important technique in improving your memory is that it battles forgetting directly and allows you to work within the bounds of your brain's capabilities. Other techniques, no less important, are about increasing encoding or storage—remember the three parts of memory are encoding, storage, and retrieval. Spaced repetition helps the last part, retrieval.

In order to commit more to memory and retain information better, space out your rehearsal and exposure to it over as long of a period as possible. In other words, you will remember something far better if you study it for one hour a day versus twenty hours in one weekend. This goes for just about everything you could possibly learn. Additional research has shown that seeing something twenty times in one day is far less effective for memory than seeing something ten times over the course of seven days.

Spaced repetition makes more sense if you imagine your brain as a muscle. Muscles can't be exercised all the time and then put back to work with little-to-no recovery. Your brain needs time to make connections between concepts, create muscle memory, and generally become familiar with something. Sleep has been shown to be where neural connections are made, and it's not just mental. Synaptic connections are formed in your brain, and dendrites are stimulated.

If an athlete works out too hard in one session like you might be tempted to in studying, one of two things will happen. The athlete will either be too exhausted, and the latter half of the workout will be useless, or the athlete will become injured. Rest and recovery are necessary to the task of learning, and sometimes effort isn't what's required.

Here's a look at what a schedule focused on spaced repetition might look like. Naturally, it's best to devise this together with your student, so that they understand exactly what they're doing and are actively engaged in planning it for themselves, according to their understanding of their own goals.

Monday at 10:00 a.m. Learn initial facts about Spanish history. You accumulate five pages of notes.

Monday at 8:00 p.m. Review notes about Spanish history, but don't just review passively. Make sure to try to recall the information from your own memory. Recalling is a much better way to process information than simply rereading and reviewing. This might only take twenty minutes.

Tuesday at 10:00 a.m. Try to recall the information without looking at your notes much. After you first try to actively recall as much as possible, go back through your notes to see what you missed, and make note of what you need to pay closer attention to. This will probably take only fifteen minutes.

Tuesday at 8:00 p.m. Review notes. This will take ten minutes.

Wednesday at 4:00 p.m. Try to independently recall the information again, and only look at your notes once you are done to see what else you have missed. This will take only ten minutes. Make sure not to skip any steps.

Thursday at 6:00 p.m. Review notes. This will take ten minutes.

Friday at 10:00 a.m. Active recall session. This will take ten minutes.

Looking at this schedule, note that you are only studying an additional seventy-five minutes throughout the week, but that you've managed to go through the entire lesson a whopping six additional times. Not only that, you've likely committed most of it to memory because you are using active recall instead of passively reviewing your notes.

You're ready for a test the next Monday. Actually, you're ready for a test by Friday afternoon. Spaced repetition gives your brain time to process concepts and make its own connections and leaps because of the repetition.

Think about what happens when you have repeated exposure to a concept. For the first couple of exposures, you may not see anything new. As you get more familiar with it and stop going through the motions, you begin to examine it on a deeper level and think about the context surrounding it. You relate it to other concepts or information, and you generally make sense of it below the surface level.

All of this, of course, is designed to push information from your short-term memory into your long-term memory. That's why cramming or studying at the last minute isn't an effective means of learning. Very little tends to make it into long-term memory because of the lack of repetition and deeper analysis. At that point, it becomes rote memorization instead of the concept learning we discussed earlier, which is destined to fade far more quickly.

When you set out to learn something, instead of measuring the number of hours you spend on it, try instead to measure the number of times you revisit the same information after the initial learning. Make it your goal to increase the frequency of reviewing, not necessarily the duration. Both matter, but the literature on spaced repetition or distributed practice makes clear that breathing room is necessary.

It's true that this type of optimal learning takes up more time and planning than most of us are used to. However, if you find yourself short on time, you can still use it strategically.

To cram for a test, exam, or other type of evaluation, we don't need material to make it fully into our long-term memory. We just need it to make it slightly past our working memory and be partially encoded into our long-term memory. We don't need to be able to recall anything the day after, so it's like we only need something to stick for a few hours.

You might not be able to do true spaced repetition if you are cramming at the last minute, but you can simulate it in a small way. Instead of studying subject X for three hours only at night, seek to study it one hour each three times a day with a few hours between each exposure.

Recall that memories need time to be encoded and stick in the brain. You are doing the best imitation of spaced repetition you can with what you have available. To get the most out of your limited studying time, study something, for example, as soon as you wake up, and then review it at noon, 4:00 p.m., and 9:00 p.m. The point is to review throughout the day and get as much repetition as possible. Remember to focus on frequency rather than duration.

During the course of your repetition, make sure to study your notes out of order to see them in different contexts and encode more effectively. Also, use active recall versus passive reading. Don't be afraid to even intersperse unrelated material to reap the benefits of interleaved practice. Make sure to focus on the underlying concepts that govern the information you are learning so you can make educated guesses about what you don't remember.

Ensure that you're reciting and rehearsing new information up to the last minute before your test. Your short-term memory can hold seven items on its best day, so you might just save yourself with a piece of information that was never going to fit into your long-term memory. It's like you're juggling. It's inevitable that you'll drop everything eventually, but it could just so happen that you're juggling something you can use. Make use of all types of memory you can consciously employ.

Spaced repetition, as you can see, approaches learning from a different perspective—in practicing retrieval and shooting for frequency as opposed to duration to improve memory. Even in situations where you don't have as much time as you'd like, you can use spaced repetition to cram for tests and overall just get more information into your brain—again, by focusing on frequency and not duration. When you spread out your learning and memorizing over a longer period of time and revisit the same material frequently, you'll be better off.

The next piece of the puzzle in better memorizing is called chunking. Unlike spaced repetition, this might be something you've heard of before, and it might even be something you currently do.

Cornell Notes

Many of the techniques covered here lend themselves well to more academic subjects, and this is certainly true of note-taking. Many of us have learnt some form of note-taking in school and college, but often this is simply mimicked behavior that we've never taken the time to properly understand. The first thing to bear in mind is that notes are not automatically necessary. But if they are, then the next thing to remember is that a note-taking method is only worth something if it genuinely aids your student to understand and retain new information. A huge mistake is to adopt some trendy or important-sounding technique that does nothing but get in the way of learning, rather than facilitate it.

This is why we spent time laying the groundwork in the previous chapter—when we understand the landscape, and our path through that landscape to reach our desired goal, it becomes far easier to pick the right tools and techniques. We don't waste time with approaches that only confuse or bore our student, but get straight to the heart of the matter with an approach that is purposeful and focused. With that caveat, let's explore some note-taking methods that have garnered fans over the years. The most famous method of note-taking is called the *Cornell method*, and elements relate to what we covered earlier. Here's how it works.

On a handwritten sheet for note-taking (writing by hand is key), split it down the middle and into two columns. Make the column on the right about twice the size as the column on the left. Label the right column "Notes" and the left column "Cues." Leave a couple inches empty at the bottom of the page and label that section "Summary."

You now have three distinct sections, but you will only be taking notes in the Notes section on the right. This is where you take normal notes on the bigger concepts with supporting detail as concisely as possible. Write everything you need to make a thorough assessment of what you're learning. Make sure to skip some space between points so you can fill in more detail and clarification at a later point. Draw charts and diagrams, make lists where appropriate, and give your best effort to capturing what matters.

You don't need to think about organization or highlighting while you are taking the initial notes. Just write what you hear or read and give as complete of a picture as possible. Record as much as possible in the right column, as you just want to capture information at this point. Don't discriminate. When you go over the notes again, you can figure out what is necessary and important.

After you're done taking notes, move on to the left Cues side. This is where, for each section or concept, you filter and analyze the Notes side and write the important parts on the Cues side.

Where the Notes side is more of a jumbled mess, the Cues side is a relatively organized account of the topic at hand—basically, the same information is on each side.

Turn five sentences of normal notes into one or two sentences with a main point and supporting facts. Hopefully you can picture it: on the left is an organized set of statements that sum everything up neatly, while on the right is a jumble of messy writing. At this point, you've already achieved the second level of taking notes as we talked about before. You've gone a level above what you normally do, and you can already skim the paper and instantly know what the notes are about.

Finally, after you're done with the Notes and Cues sides, move to the Summary section at the bottom.

This is where you attempt to summarize everything you've just taken notes on into a few top-level ideas and statements, with only the important supporting facts or exceptions to the rules. You want to say as much in as few words as possible because, when you review your notes, you should be able to understand quickly and not have to deconstruct and analyze all over again.

Your goal is to be able to skim the Summary and Cues section and move on. Where you previously had one page full of messy notes, now you have a short Summary section where you can instantly gain understanding of new information. It also allows you to memorize more effectively, as again it's just a few sentences versus a page you would have to analyze every time. And once again, synthesizing for one more repetition doesn't hurt.

As a quick example, why we don't we review what we've been talking about in this lesson? Suppose we are taking Cornell notes on this concept itself. On the right side will be as much as you can capture. It won't be verbatim, and you'll probably need to write in short phrases.

But it is not too organized—it's just a mass of information based on what you've heard. On the left side, you'll have a few shorter phrases, such as the four stages of notes and what happens in each stage, how Cornell notes function, and their importance in learning more effectively.

As for the Summary section, you would boil everything you've learned from this lesson down into one or two sentences—there are four stages of learning: taking notes, editing, analysis, reflection. Cornell notes force you to go through all four stages and help you organize information better with three sections to enforce information.

In completing this process, you have created your own study guide. Better yet, you also have the entire process you used to create it documented on the same page, from original notes to synthesis and summarization. You have a record of information that allows you to go as deep as you want or refer to whatever you wish. The most important part is that you've created something that has personal significance to you because you've phrased everything in a way in which you derive meaning. You are making the information fit your mental scheme, not the other way around.

Overall, taking notes is not a lazy, passive activity. That's the real secret of great notes. They are intended to serve as something you can refer to, instantly understand, and find helpful, as opposed to having to decipher them. This won't work if you have to first try to understand someone else's sense of structure and organization.

Peter Brown, author of the book *Make It Stick*, simplifies this point on notes: he maintains that when no effort is put into the learning process, it doesn't last very long.

In one study Brown cited, students were allowed to copy notes word for word on some material but were asked to rephrase *other* material in their own words. When these students were tested later, they did a far better job of recalling the material they had paraphrased themselves.

It may be convenient—for the students, if not the professor—to provide written notes for lectures. But the lack of effort inherent in this arrangement will handicap the student. In fact, the less effort and involvement a student is able to use to get by, the worse the learning will be.

Your notes are how your brain will process, understand, and memorize information. That means you need to make sure you have a good foundation to start with.

The final best practice on interacting with information for self-learners is the art of self-explanation. Again, you may recognize elements of this from the SQ3R method, specifically the part about *recitation*.

How to use Purposeful Annotation

One final technique we'll look at in this chapter involves not just "close reading" and annotation, but *purposeful* annotation. Again, this depends greatly on the material you're trying to teach and the skills, age and personality of your student. Have you ever sat down to read something and just kind of... let your eyes go over the page without any of it really sinking in? Reading is actually a very active process, and requires a constant back and forth between the material on the page and your absorption and comprehension of that information.

More than this, reading is not just an isolated activity—it's always embedded in some bigger picture. Without understanding this bigger picture, reading can seem a bit pointless and unfocused. If written texts form a big part of what you're trying to teach, then there's no way around it: you'll have to also teach a method for *how* to read, according to your purposes.

Simply picking up a book and reading it is one thing. But an effective reader reads with *purpose*. Purpose means knowing **why** you are reading something; to put it another way, you need a clear idea of what you intend to do with the information after you've gathered it from the text. How exactly does it align with your stated goals and aims?

Many college students sit down with a textbook in one hand and a highlighter in another, highlighting sections as they go, with no idea of why they've chosen this method, or what they hope to achieve from it. This is precisely the method that will leave you thinking, "wait, what did I just read?" at the end of it!

When your student annotates (i.e. makes highlights, or adds symbols or notes on the text or margins as they read) they need to be doing so toward a pre-identified purpose. A simple way to bring more purpose into any reading is to deliberately ask, "Why am I reading this?" Pause and prime your student to look for pertinent information by setting a reading goal **before** they actually read. This can also be done by alerting them to the task they'll have to complete **afterwards**, i.e. a summary, an analysis, or a comprehension question. This shapes and guides their focus as they read—it gives purpose.

Think of reading as a conversation you're having with the text—you need to respond intelligently and increase your *understanding* of the material. If you were talking to a person and you got confused, you might ask them to repeat themselves, to rephrase things, or you'd ask a question to ensure you understood what they were saying. Teach your student to read in the same way, to be attentive and respond to what they read, and engage with the text by making summaries, connections, analyses or even arguments *as they read it.*

So, we need to encourage our students to engage with texts before, during and after reading. Before, they can set goals and intentions; during, they can make meaningful notes and annotations; and after, they can perform some task to cement and apply what they've read. For a simple example, you might give your student an article and pique their curiosity by saying that this author was heavily criticized for the argument they made, and can they guess why? Then, on reading, ask your student to tease out the logical structure of the argument the author is making, plus any response they have—i.e., what do they think of the author's stance?

Finally, after reading, you can ask your student to not only summarize what they've read but take a look at your question again: What did they make of the author's argument? You could then give them another article, one refuting the first, to add even more depth to the topic. As you can see, at no point are you ever just reading for the sake of it—rather, your reading is targeted to a specific goal.

When we read this way, annotations become tools, or even breadcrumbs that enable us to quickly find our way into and out of concepts. The truth is that many students, of all ages, don't have a natural inclination to read something unless they can see some relevance to their own lives, or the tasks they're trying to achieve for themselves. In a way, active engagement with new information *is the same thing as* learning—without consciously being present to focus and direct attention, how could we be said to learn anything?

Annotations should reflect an *inner* cognitive engagement. When your student writes a question or rebuttal in the margin of a text, it should be because that thought genuinely occurred to them, and they want to make a note of it, rather than them thinking, "Well, I should probably take some notes or something, here looks like the right place to make something up."

It's important for you as the teacher to understand your broader aims so you can set the stage for the student. If you want them to absorb the information in general, focus on making a summary or simple outline. If you want them to engage more meaningfully with the material itself, ask them to analyze the content more closely. If you want to make sure they actually understand the points rather than just memorize them, ask them comprehension questions, or to paraphrase. Have in mind one or two clearly defined verbs to guide your student: *analyze, compare, organize, integrate, describe, summarize, explain* or *develop* are all verbs that ask your student to take an active stance when reading.

Once they know what they're doing, students can decide what annotation will work best. Questions in the margins? Highlighting? Circling new words and finding their definitions? Underlining the direct quotes in a text? None of these approaches is better or worse than the next—what matters is that the annotation is logically supporting the purpose of reading. There's no need to get bogged down in specific annotation rules, color-coded pens, special symbols, etc. In fact, a system your student devises entirely on their own is likely to be far more effective.

Your goal as a teacher is to guide your student to a place where they feel empowered, confident, and curious enough to take a hold of the reading process and direct it themselves. Everything in service of a purpose is more energized and clearer—reading is no exception. You may find that setting a reading task in the right way naturally leads to students annotating. Your only prompt might be to suggest they write their goal in big letters at the top of the page, and see what happens.

Remember, the point is not to generate pretty notes, but to facilitate the inner cognitive processes that come with true understanding. You want to *internalize* the slow, deliberate process of engagement with new material. One more good idea: ask your student to actively evaluate how well their note-taking and annotating systems are working. How have they helped? Have they helped? This guides them to think more deeply in the future about how they want to connect with the text.

Takeaways

- There are a range of practical methods to help on the learning journey. The SQ3R method is a way to shape the learning process, via Survey (gain an overview of the material), Question (develop deeper understanding by asking questions to direct your learning), Read (active, careful intake of the material or information), Recite (drill what has been learnt to organize and cement it in your mind) and Review (assess your progress as compared to the start, and according to your overall goals).

- Bloom's taxonomy explains that mastery is cumulative, and proceeds through levels of deepening understanding. These are Remember, Understand, Apply, Analyze, Evaluate, and Create. Each of these levels of engagement depends on mastery of the previous level. As a teacher, you can shape progressive challenge by bearing these stages in mind.

- Spaced repetition or distributed practice is a way to strengthen memory and recall. The idea is to recite or review material at frequent intervals spaced over as long a period as possible, rather than "cramming" all at once, which is less effective. The key is consistency and spaced-out practice, which allows students to practice recall itself.

- The Cornell Method of note-taking teaches your student to take natural notes, but then later distill key themes and points from those notes and then summarize their main findings, essentially generating a concept map of the material. This improves not only retention but depth understanding.

- Finally, purposeful annotation is something done during reading, but in reality occurs before, during and after reading. Reading should be active and directed; you need to know beforehand why you are reading and what you intend to do with the information after you've read. This knowledge primes and focuses reading, and makes it easier to choose annotation methods (highlighting, notes, symbols, etc.) that work in context.

Chapter 4. Advanced Techniques

Our previous chapter covered some possibly familiar ground, i.e. how a student can work "smarter not harder" and use a range of cognitive tools in the most efficient, logical and satisfying way. In this chapter, we're going a little further and looking at approaches and techniques that delve deeper.

Here, we'll be extending beyond the usual classroom-based techniques and looking more philosophically at the process of acquiring knowledge itself. What does it really mean to be someone's guide, mentor, trainer? How can we exploit a more sophisticated understanding of how this strange thing called Learning (capital L!) really works, for ourselves and for our students?

Problem-Based Learning

There is an urban legend about novice metalworkers. Their teachers tell them to carve a complex structure out of a solid block of metal with only hand tools at their disposal. After they complete this tedious and seemingly impossible problem, what do you suppose was accomplished by the student? They became true experts with hand tools.

What about famous Mr. Miyagi from the *Karate Kid* movie? Who can forget how he taught his student, Daniel-san, how to perform hard labor? And yet, after this goal was achieved, it turned out Daniel-san learned the basics of karate.

Through solving a problem or reaching for a goal, learning was made inevitable.

Problem-based learning (PBL) is where you start with a problem that needs to be solved, and you force learning through the process of solving that problem. You try to accomplish a goal that necessitates learning. Instead of setting out to learn X, the idea is to set a goal of solving problem Y, and in the process, learning X. Of course, this is pure learning transfer.

Usually, we learn information and skills in a linear manner. In school, a traditional approach is commonly used: material is given to us, we memorize it, and we are shown how that information solves a problem. This might even be how you structure your learning when you're by yourself—because you don't know anything different.

PBL requires you to identify what you already know about the problem and what knowledge and resources you still need, to figure out how and where to obtain that new information, and finally how to piece together a solution to the problem. This is far different from the linear approach of most schooling. We can draw on my failed romantic escapades as an adolescent for illustration.

I wanted to impress Jessica from Spanish class. It's a noble and mighty motivation that has been the impetus for many changes in the life of a young (and old) male. We were in the same Spanish class, and I had the good fortune of sitting directly behind her. It turns out she wasn't too interested in Spanish, so she would constantly turn around and ask me for help.

I would first get caught in her eyes, but then my spirits would fall because I realized I had no idea how to answer her questions. What if she started asking the other guys in the class? I didn't want that!

With that in mind, I began to study and learn Spanish so she would have all the more reason to continue turning around and talking to me. It's amazing what you can do when you have the proper motivation for it, and I probably became fluent more quickly than anyone in the class that year. What's more, I would look up obscure or complex phrases solely to impress her, just in case I had the opportunity.

I created a massive set of flashcards. They started with one word on the back of each card, but by the end of the school year, they had three to four sentences on the back of each, all in Spanish. I got an A+ in the class, one of the few in my high school career, but I never did get anywhere with Jessica.

This is a classic case of PBL—I wanted to solve the problem of X (Jessica), but I ended up learning Y (Spanish) in the process.

Of course, the key is to be deliberate about the problem you spend your time solving, so what you learn helps you accomplish what you want. It can be as simple as wanting to master a new scale on the guitar, and attempting to play a difficult song that incorporates that scale. You can see how focusing on solving a problem can be more helpful and educational than simply reading a textbook or hearing a lecture. There's certainly something to be said for firsthand experience.

PBL has been around in one form or another since John Dewey's pivotal 1916 book *Democracy and Education: An Introduction to the Philosophy of Education.* One of the basic premises of Dewey's book was learning by doing.

Fast forward to the 1960s, when PBL had its modern start. Medical schools started using real patient cases and examples to train future doctors. Indeed, this is still how many medical students learn to diagnose and treat patients. Rather than memorize an endless supply of facts and figures, medical students went through the diagnostic process and picked up information along the way. That's exercising a different muscle than reading and writing notes.

What questions should they ask of the patient? What information do they need from the patient? What tests should be run? What do the results of those tests mean? How do the results determine the course of treatment? By asking and answering all of these questions in the process of PBL, medical students ultimately learn how to treat patients.

Imagine that a medical student is presented with the following case: A sixty-six-year-old male patient comes in to the office complaining of recent shortness of breath. What are the next steps in this blank canvas?

In addition to medical, family, and social histories, the student would want to find out how long the symptoms have been occurring, at what time of day, what activities lead to shortness of breath, and whether anything makes it worse or better. The physical exam, then, becomes problem-focused: check blood pressure, listen to heart and lungs, check legs for edema, etc. Next the student would determine whether any lab tests or X-rays need to be done. And then based on those results, the student would come up with a plan for treatment. And that's just for starters.

If the instructor wanted the student to learn about how to deal with potential heart problems, they accomplished that. By applying their investigative skills to real-world cases, the learning was more realistic, more memorable, and more engaging for the medical students. Research has shown that when learning is problem-based for medical students, clinical reasoning and problem-solving skills improve, learning is more in-depth, and concepts are integrated for better overall understanding of the material.

PBL forces students to take ownership of the solution and approach, and they absorb a concept or set of information in an entirely different manner. Instead of simply solving for X, they must come up with the entire equation that leads to X. It involves a deep sense of exploration and analysis, both of which lead to a greater understanding than simple regurgitation.

PBL leads to greater self-motivation as well because rather than learning for learning's sake, there is a real-life issue at stake, with real-life consequences.

Living in the "real world," we typically aren't given case scenarios or assigned to group projects (at least not in the elementary-school sense of the phrase) to assist in our learning goals. Whether we know it or not, we can put ourselves in a position to enhance our learning by directing it to specific purposes. What follows are a few examples of how to find a problem that will necessitate further learning on your part.

Meal Planning. For instance, you want to solve a problem of dealing with delayed and frantic dinners. You choose this task because, besides solving the problem of unnecessary stress and anxiety, you will learn how to become a better cook in every sense of the word. You want to solve X (stressful meals) but along the way also learn Y (how to cook better).

So, what steps would you take to become more proficient in the kitchen? One way would be to implement a meal-planning system to allow you to try new recipes and techniques. First, determine what do you already know about the problem? Your family needs to eat. Recipes would be nice, perhaps starting out easy and then becoming more involved. You need the ingredients to make those recipes, a schedule of what meal to serve when, and a strategy for how you will tackle the more advanced techniques.

What do you still need to know? You need actual recipes and ingredient lists. You need some sort of organized plan for when you'll serve each dinner, probably a calendar. You may want to identify specific skills you want to acquire.

Where will you obtain new information to help solve this problem? Maybe you start by asking members of your family to share their three favorite meals with you. Then you hop on Pinterest to find some recipes. From there, you make a grocery list, maybe on a notepad, or your computer in a Word doc, or a grocery app you find. Next you need to put your meals onto a calendar. Again, you may do this on your computer, or you might find a meal-planning printable or app. And maybe you want to explore online grocery ordering with delivery or pickup to further save time (and probably impulse spending). You'll need to figure out how you will learn new cooking approaches: reading, YouTube videos, going to a class, etc.

By making a strategic plan to enhance your cooking skills, you have solved your mealtime chaos by using PBL! You identified what you already knew (you need ideas about what new skills you wanted to learn, meal ideas, recipes, a grocery list), figured out what you still needed to know (the techniques themselves, specific recipes, ingredient lists, a meal calendar), and where you found that information (family, Pinterest, apps, books, online, computer, etc.).

Not only have you created a plan for your family's upcoming meals, you have devised a strategy to use moving forward week after week, month after month, all the while learning new techniques and improving your cooking skills. By developing a meal-planning strategy, you are saving time and money, and you may see a decrease in chaos and an increase in family satisfaction with meals. Call it killing two birds with one stone.

The Broken Toaster. Let's consider a more complicated problem. Your toaster seems to no longer be working, and you have toast for breakfast every day. You've always wanted to learn more about electronics and put to use what you learned years ago. You want to solve X (broken toaster) but along the way also learn Y (basic electronics skills). What would PBL look like in this somewhat daunting scenario?

The first step is to determine what you already know. Your toaster isn't functioning. You're pretty handy and would consider fixing it yourself. You know a little about wiring. And you really like your toaster, a model that is no longer made.

What, then, do you need to know to solve this problem? You will need to determine the specific cause of your toaster malfunction. You will potentially require some instruction for aspects of the problem outside your current skill set. You will need tools and supplies as well as the time and a place to work on your toaster.

In the information-gathering stage, you will disassemble your toaster to try to determine the problem. You may look online or go to the library for a "fix-it" manual for small appliances. There are YouTube videos you could consult for a visual tutorial. Then, once you've determined the issue, learned how to fix it, and made the repair, you're back in business with your toaster.

Problem-based learning provides a helpful framework for a thoughtful, organized way to approach a problem, challenge, or dilemma in order to learn a new skill or information. You can think of PBL as a series of steps as demonstrated in the examples above.

Define your problem.
Determine what you already know.
List potential solutions and choose the one most likely to succeed.

Break the steps into action items (a timeline often helps).
Identify what you still need to know and how you will get that information.

There are some distinct advantages to PBL. Not only will you have better retention of what you have learned, you will generally gain a deeper understanding of the problem and solutions than if you had taken a less focused approach. While it can seem like a problem-based approach has too many steps and will take too long, generally PBL tends to save you time in the long run since you aren't randomly trying less-well-thought-out solution after solution. Planning and formulating a systematic plan ultimately saves you time, and often money, too! That is the benefit of directly solving a problem—you get to the heart of what matters.

PBL can be applied to most any aspect of your life. You may have to get creative in how to design a problem or goal around something you want to learn, but this is the type of learning technique that will skyrocket your progress. After all, there's only so much we can gain without applying what we know to the real world via learning transfer.

Socrates the Great

The importance of being a question master cannot be overstated; it's not about being pedantic or provocative. We've said multiple times that you can't expect information to teach you or to make itself understood. This responsibility will always fall upon you in the end. If you're not getting or understanding something from a lecture, book, or video, the answer surely cannot be to keep reading the same passage over and over.

You must make an effort to investigate and pull understanding out yourself. Or, if you're playing the role of the teacher, you need to set up the exact environmental conditions to allow this process to best unfold in your student, and prompt them and prime them so they are doing more than just going through the motions. It makes you think of psychology experiments where rats continue to shock themselves by pressing a lever. No progress is being made, so obviously the approach needs to change. It's a clear example of working smarter, not harder; no one can deny that the rat works hard, but with questionable results.

Let's consider two people who read the same book on Spanish history. Jimbo will read along and review the information. He will take notes and can pass a test quite easily on the subject. His answers read like bullet points for a recipe for cornbread. He receives a B+. Kudos for Jimbo.

Kunal, on the other hand, reads the same book, but he only does this once or twice, and instead spends the rest of his time trying to gain a deeper understanding of the whys and motivations of Spanish conquistadors and kings. He attains an A+ on the same test, a better mark because he displayed a deeper insight than Jimbo could ever possess. His answers are more like essays, and even though he forgot a couple minute details, he made insightful leaps of reasoning and judgment because of his deeper understanding.

He achieved this level of mastery by asking probing questions and using them to get behind facts and information. He processed the information and chewed on it with his questions. He finds that he doesn't even need to know all the facts if he asks the right questions, because he can predict what the conquistadors would probably have done. Kudos for Kunal.

In learning, it is said that answers are far less important than the questions people ask.

Indeed, we've also heard this advice in relation to job interviews, where you should always have "intelligent questions" to display that you understand the interviewing company on a deeper level.

Rote memorization of information is sometimes the goal, but if we ever want to understand and comprehend more deeply, questions are the first place to start. Questions will take a flat piece of information and turn it into a living, three-dimensional piece of knowledge that interacts with the world at large. That is the reality of any fact or piece of information; it has a story we are usually overlooking in the interest of speed or efficiency. To ask a question is to see a subject, identify what you don't know, and also be open to the fact that your entire understanding could be wrong. Meaningful learning only occurs when you understand what surrounds information, such as the background and context.

Put another way, good questions end up allowing us to *triangulate* understanding. Take a textbook, for example. It is necessarily broad and cannot hope to cover all the subtleties involved. If we fully accept what we read, then we are set on a singular path. If we ask questions, we are able to see that the path itself contains twists and turns and may not even be accurate. Different lines of inquiry are generated, and it is understood that there are multiple paths, each with their own perspective. Questions allow us to both clarify misunderstandings and reinforce what we already know. In the end, we come to an understanding of the same textbook that is nuanced and more accurate.

Luckily for us, teachers have known this for literally thousands of years. The most helpful framework for generating insightful questions comes from none other than Socrates himself, the ancient Greek philosopher perhaps best known for being Plato's teacher, as well as being executed by the state for "corrupting the minds of the youth." His method of teaching was largely in the form of dialogues and questions, appropriately called the *Socratic Method*.

When you boil it down, the Socratic Method is when you ask questions upon questions in an effort to dissect an assertion or statement for greater understanding. The person asking the questions might seem like they are on the offensive, but they are asking questions to enrich both parties and discover the underlying assumptions and motivations of the assertion or statement. It is from this process that we have a framework for effective questioning.

Imagine that you make a proclamation, and the only response you get is a smug, "Oh, is that so? What about X and Y?" Unfortunately, the know-it-all questioner is on the right path.

American law schools are notorious for using the Socratic Method. A professor will ask a student a question, and then the student will have to defend their statement against a professor's questioning regarding the merits of a case or law. It's not adversarial by nature, but it does force someone to explain their reasoning and logic—and of course, gaps in knowledge and logical flaws will probably surface. This process serves the goal of deeper understanding and insight. It may cause defensiveness, though it is not offensive in itself.

So what exactly is the Socratic Method, beyond asking a series of tough questions that make people uncomfortable? When you do it to yourself, you are forcing understanding. You are putting yourself through an incredible stress test that will make you question yourself and your logic. It will force you to discard your assumptions and see what you might be

131

missing. If you are mercilessly questioned and picked apart with Socratic questioning, what remains afterward will be deeply comprehended and validated. If there is an error in your thinking or a gap in your understanding, it will be found, corrected, and proofed with a rebuttal. That's deep learning.

As a brief example, imagine you are telling someone that the sky is blue.

This seems like an unquestionable statement that is an easy truth. Obviously, the sky is blue. You've known that since you were a child. You go outside and witness it each day. You've told someone that their eyes were as blue as the sky. But remember, our goal with questions is to better acquire knowledge as to the sky's blueness. So imagine someone asks *why* you know it is blue.

There are many ways to answer that question, but you decide to say that you know the sky is blue because it reflects the ocean, and that the ocean is blue, even though this is erroneous. The questioner asks how you know it is a reflection of the ocean.

How would you answer this?

This brief line of Socratic questioning just revealed that you have no idea why or how the sky reflects (or doesn't) the blue of the planet's oceans. You just attempted to explain an underlying assumption, and you were mildly surprised to discover that you had no idea.

That, in a nutshell, is the importance of the Socratic Method. A series of innocent and simple questions directed at yourself, honestly and earnestly answered, can unravel what you thought you knew and lead you to understand exactly what you don't know. This is often just as important as knowing what you *do* know because it uncovers your blind spots and weaknesses. Recall that the method was used by teachers as a teaching tool, so it is designed to impart deeper understanding and clarify ambiguities.

There are six types of Socratic questions as delineated by R.W. Paul. After just briefly glancing at this list, you might understand how these questions can improve your learning and lead you to fill in the gaps in your knowledge.

The six types of questions are:
1. Clarification questions—why exactly does it matter?

2. Probing assumptions—what hidden assumptions might exist?
3. Probing rationale, reasons, evidence—what proven evidence exists?
4. Questioning viewpoints and perspectives—what other perspectives exist?
5. Probing implications and consequences—what does this mean, what is the significance, and how does it connect to other information?
6. Questions about the question—why is this question important?

Clarification questions: What is the real meaning of what is being said? Is there an underlying hidden motivation or significance to this piece of information? What do they hope to achieve with it? Suppose we have the same assertion from above, where the sky is blue. Here are some sample questions from each category you could plausibly ask to gain clarity and challenge their thoughts.

- What does it matter to you if the sky is blue?
- What is the significance to you?
- What is the main issue here?
- What exactly do you mean by that?
- What does that have to do with the rest of the discussion?
- Why would you say that?

Probing assumptions: What assumptions are the assertions based on, and are they actually supported by evidence? What is opinion and belief, and what is evidence-based fact or proven in some other way? Unless you are reading a scientific paper, there are always inherent assumptions that may or may not be accurate.

- Is your blue my blue?
- Why do you think the sky is blue?
- How can you prove or verify that?
- Where is this coming from exactly?
- So what leads you to believe the sky is blue?
- How can you prove that the sky is blue?

Probing rationale, reasons, and evidence: How do you know the evidence is trustworthy and valid? What are the conclusions drawn, and what rationale, reasons, and evidence are specifically used in such a way? What might be missing or glazed over?

- What's the evidence for the sky's color, and why is it convincing?
- How exactly does the ocean's reflection color the sky?
- What is an example of that?
- Why do you think that is true?
- What if the information was incorrect or flawed?
- Can you tell me the reasoning?

135

Questioning viewpoints and perspectives: People will almost always present an assertion or argument from a specific bias, so play the devil's advocate and remain skeptical about what they have come up with. Ask why opposing viewpoints and perspectives aren't preferred and why they don't work.

- How else could your evidence be interpreted, an alternative view?
- Why is that research the best in proving that the sky is blue?
- Could the same be said about proving the sky is red? Why or why not?
- What are the potential flaws in this argument?
- What is the counterargument?
- Why doesn't the sky color the ocean instead of the other way around?

Probing implications and consequences: What are the conclusions and why? What else could it mean, and why was this particular conclusion drawn? What will happen as a consequence, and why?

- If the sky is blue, what does that mean about reflections?
- Who is affected by the sky's color?
- What does this information mean, and what are the consequences?

136

- What does this finding imply? What else does it determine?
- How does it connect to the broader topic or narrative?
- If the sky is blue, what does that mean about the ocean?
- What else could your evidence and research prove about the planet?

Questions about the question: This is less effective when you are directing this question to yourself. Directed toward someone else, you are forcing people to ponder why you asked the question or why you went down that line of questioning, and realize that you had something you wanted to evoke. What did you mean when you said that, and why did you ask about X rather than Y?

- So why do you think I asked you about your belief in the sky's color?
- What do you think I wanted to do when I asked you about this?
- How do you think this knowledge might help you in other topics?
- How does this apply to everyday life and what we were discussing earlier?

At first, it sounds like a broken record, but there is a method to the madness. Each question may seem similar, but if answered correctly and adequately, they go in different directions. In the example of the blue sky, there are over twenty separate questions—twenty separate answers and probes into someone's simple assertion that the sky is blue. You can almost imagine how someone might discover that they know next to nothing and are only able to regurgitate a limited set of facts without context or understanding.

You can apply the Socratic Method to ensure that you are understanding what you think you are. You can think of it as a systematic process of examining and just double-checking yourself. The end result will always be a win, as you either confirm your mastery or figure out exactly what is missing.

Suppose you hear from a friend that the Spanish Inquisition was a fairly humane process of light interrogation, with only minor maimings and lashings (various sources put the death toll at, on average, around one hundred thousand people). In this instance, you can use the Socratic questions to correct a mistake. The six question types, as a reminder:
1. Clarification questions—why does it matter?
2. Probing assumptions—what hidden assumptions might exist?

3. Probing rationale, reasons, evidence—what proven evidence exists?
4. Questioning viewpoints and perspectives—what other perspectives exist?
5. Probing implications and consequences—what does this mean, what is the significance, and how does it connect to other information?
6. Questions about the question—why is this question important?

To check the veracity of this statement, you might ask:

- What exactly is being said, and why does it matter?
- What is that statement based on?
- What makes you think it is true? Where's the evidence for it?
- Who might have this perspective, and why? What might be the opposing perspective? Why is that?
- What does this mean for Spanish history as a whole? Are all history textbooks incorrect? What else will be affected by this knowledge?
- Why do you think I might be asking you about this?

What about using the Socratic questions for deeper understanding of a topic, such as the biology of the brain? Actually, the questions don't change—all six of the above questions can be used in the same way to more deeply understand brain structures. You'll learn, you'll poke holes, and you'll understand. Isn't that what this whole thing is all about?

Critical Thinking Pro

If you've ever followed the Socratic method in any shape or form, congratulations, you have inadvertently practiced critical thinking. You'll recognize this broad technique as one of the five pedagogical approaches we covered early in the book, i.e. the inquiry-based approach. In taking this stance with a student, you are in effect modeling for them the internal process that they will one day perform for themselves, long after you have stopped teaching them. A critical thinker has an internalized teacher in their brain, asking thoughtful questions, pointing out inconsistencies, and regularly asking, "So what are we doing here? What's this? What does that really mean anyway?"

Nobody likes to think of themselves as a poor or sloppy thinker, but being honest about the *quality* of your thought processes is a necessary first step to true learning. Our previous chapter focused on content and methods of absorption, organization, retention and so on. But critical thinking is about the *how* of learning, rather than the *what*. Critical thinking doesn't refer to something we are, but something we do. It's an approach that, when practiced often enough, improves not only the quality and strength of our thoughts, but makes us experts at learning, period.

Sounds good. So, what does critical thinking look like on the ground? You've seen it already with the Socratic Method—i.e. the principle of taking nothing for granted. When you ask a question, you immediately put yourself in the position of not knowing the answer, i.e. not assuming anything. Making no assumptions, you open the way for deeper insight. This is the attitude that powers the scientific method, and feeds on sincere curiosity.

As a teacher, encourage this skill by keeping yourself out of the picture as much as possible. Instead of handing your student pre-formed and fixed opinions, give them only a question to spur their own interest, allowing them to arrive at conclusions on their own. Of course there is a part of teaching that consists of instruction and explanation. But try not to tell your student what to think—it's always better to support the student's individual process of working out what *they* think. Invite your student to challenge any and all assumptions—even those that frame the parameters of your learning relationship.

Doing this positions your student at the center of the learning inquiry, and puts them in charge of their own development and understanding. Your goal is never to cram your student's head full of all the things you believe they need to know, but to help them achieve the kind of conscious, mature open-mindedness that lets them pursue their own content, according to their own faculties.

This is not the same as blandly permitting students to hold whatever poorly considered opinion they want to—in the arena of learning, every thought, opinion or claim needs to earn its keep. This means that we are not afraid to challenge bias and assumption, but on the other hand, we also keep a neutral perspective and suspend judgment until we have good enough reason to hold on to any one claim over another.

You can model this attitude for your student by keeping your own ego-based bias in check. Show them that revising your beliefs when faced with new evidence is simply part of the process, by being comfortable with doing it yourself. Teachers can be incredibly stubborn and closed-minded, since they are so used to occupying a position of unchallenged authority and correctness. You can go a long way by proactively engaging with your own blind spots, however, and you'll likely gain your students' trust and respect in the process.

The attitude needn't be combative or hostile— it's never an embarrassment to make an error on the way to learning, and there's no shame in adjusting your position if that's where your understanding takes you. In fact, one of the greatest lessons any teacher can impart is that this process is indistinguishable from learning itself, and that truly intelligent people never fear mistakes, ignorance or being proved wrong.

This is what many call a "growth mindset," and it takes fear, bias and ego out of the picture and places data and knowledge at the center. All humans have beliefs, preferences, expectations, flaws in thinking, and unique personal histories. But being a critical thinker means deliberately separating facts and logic from personal belief. It's a mark of a very sophisticated thinker to say, "Well, for personal reasons I would love it if XYZ were true, but I can't deny the evidence to the contrary, so I guess I must have been wrong on this count."

Critical thinkers never see an idea or belief as a permanent place to stay, forever and ever. They don't view ideas or thoughts like a favorite football team that they support regardless of circumstance, out of loyalty or stubbornness or a righteous feeling that they are on the right "side" of things. Rather, thoughts and ideas are constantly changed and updated, as learning progresses. Abandoning some ideas is not seen as weakness or error, but simply accumulating more data, and a step on the path to better understanding—which is always, always the goal.

No matter what your student is learning, as a teacher you can encourage this spirit of open, critical examination by never shutting down any earnest inquiry, and always welcoming debate and analysis. Support and validate students when they recognize a fault in their own logic, but refrain from praising any idea over another. Your goal is not really to find the "right answer," but to cultivate a sound path on the way. After all, you don't even necessarily have to pick a side or make a final pronouncement. Remind yourself and your student that it's always possible to say, "I don't know," or perhaps "I don't know *yet*." It's more mature to acknowledge the complexity of an unresolved and messy situation than to force a conclusion that oversimplifies it, just to satisfy the ego.

In real life, there are seldom neat, easy answers, but you can teach your student to tolerate a certain degree of nuance, and to hold an idea without needing to force a decision, or hurry to attach opinions and emotions to it. Critical thinking is a hallmark of metacognition—we learn to not only work within our own mental models, but to stand outside them and ask with neutrality whether they are working, and how, and if something better could be used instead.

Naturally, communicating the power of critical thinking to others requires a skilled teacher who is able to think critically themselves. Teach your student that there are always opportunities for self-reflection, for questioning, for rooting out bias, and for examining what is being overlooked—and the best way to do this is to practice it yourself, as you teach.

Putting it All Together

Having said all this, let's remind ourselves that teaching, to be effective, needs to continually come back to the concrete. We need to work from abstract principles, but at some point, we also need to anchor in action. Inside the right theoretical framework, even the simplest and most unassuming "activity" suddenly takes on a new light. Let us look closely at a few teaching strategies, whether in a more formal classroom, alone or with a partner, so we can see how to use them to gauge understanding, offer explanation, ask questions and give valuable feedback.

As you read through these and decide if you'd like to use them for your particular purposes, keep in mind that the preferred technique or activity is always the one that best allows your student to really understand the material. If it doesn't work, just drop it, or adapt it until it does! Remember that these are all intended to be interactive, dynamic and adjustable exercises that allow you to help your students' natural learning process.

Think-pair-share
If it works for your situation, have your students think about a task alone at first, then share their findings and responses with a partner, and then finally share that combined

knowledge with the larger group. This encourages comparative and collaborative thinking, supports debate and discussion, and allows students to see aspects they might not have considered before. This technique is ideal for smaller groups. When used with larger groups, you end up spending too much time on discussion surrounding potentially wrong answers, leaving little time for actual teaching.

Use "mini quizzes"
No, this isn't to test the content itself, but to reflect on and appraise the learning process. At the end of the lesson, ask the student to take a moment to write down the main thing they learnt, one thing they still have difficulty with, plus any questions they have. This focuses learning and allows you to structure your next lesson according to their current understanding, as well as encouraging active self-reflection.

Recruit student teachers
We've already seen how useful it can be to get a student with a more advanced skillset to teach and guide a student with a less developed one. A great way to formalize this process is to break your lesson down into chunks, and then assign these chunks to smaller groups of students, so each is tasked with understanding

just one part of the whole. Then, shuffle the groups around so that students have to pass their knowledge on to each other and see where the new information fits in with theirs.

Students are thus both teachers of what they know and also students trying to understand what others know. The result is a deeper, more thorough understanding of the elements of a bigger picture. This is a great technique for allowing students to find their own causal connections and meaningful links in a greater system, instead of you outlining it for them directly.

Another way to deploy this method, if permitted by your institution, is having a student teaching assistant who holds regular interactions with your class. They can sometimes contextualize information for other students more effectively than professors themselves because the assistant has had more recent experience as a student. You can also use the assistant to give your students an introduction to concepts you're going to teach while you handle the complex parts yourself.

Assign a project
Frame your student's activity as a project that they direct and piece together, with your

feedback and guidance. Whether you ask them to create a speech, presentation or essay, take the opportunity to assess their process, pose thoughtful questions or give feedback. This works well with real-world tasks that have a strong practical element. You can then ask the students themselves to determine a rubric to grade their project, and think of ways to measure their own performance against project outcomes.

Use essays or debate

You could focus your lesson around a single prompt or question and then get one or more students to respond with an essay or argument of their own. They can present or submit this piece or else actively engage in discussion or debate with other students. You might also ask students to grade and rate example pieces, before or after they create one themselves. Alternatively, you can divide the class into several groups, assign a position on the question to each and ask them to defend it. This strengthens their ability to think critically about the logical structure of arguments, and see a model for how to organize their own attempts.

Encourage synthesis

Remember that learning is all about making meaningful connections. Encourage students to synthesize material from two different sources; for example, you could ask them to connect a discussion with the material covered in a textbook, or compare and contrast material from two very different books to arrive at a third, unique perspective. This will really allow you to see where your student is in terms of understanding the material, and you can quickly find gaps in comprehension. It's also a perfect way to encourage students to "think for themselves" on the more complex consequences and implications of the material they're encountering.

This method is particularly useful for teaching social sciences because different theorists have their own unique conceptions of things. If you were to ask three philosophers the meaning of life, they will give you very different answers that are based on different understandings of what life is. By comparing several of these disparate frameworks, students can gain a holistic understanding of the one concept they are all discussing.

Use observation
You could ask students to spend some time watching an interaction, discussion or activity

and have them respond by taking notes, asking questions or offering their own analysis and interpretation. In this way, other students' work can become data to unpack and examine.

By asking your student to silently observe something, you are targeting their attention which you can then focus on making summaries or outlines. You could, for example, have some students engage in a debate and ask the other students to observe and evaluate their strategies. By doing so, you've added extra dimensions to what might otherwise be a very static and uninteresting process.

What all of these methods have in common is that they:

a. Allow your student/s to work interactively and proactively
b. Give you the chance to gauge their deeper understanding
c. Create an opportunity for you to give meaningful feedback

Bearing in mind the scientific, open-minded, Socratic approach to learning, you can use one or more of these activities as a platform to support and evaluate the learning process on a deeper level. The above are focused primarily on interactive group or pair work, and their strength is in how they encourage your student to communicate dynamically, compare with others, and develop their own understanding through self-explanation.

Naturally, you might only have one student or be teaching a topic that doesn't lend itself well to group work. In that case, you'll want to draw on more visual activities instead. Both group work and visual representations, however, are simply there to give you the opportunity to *see* your student's internal thinking made external, so you can gauge their level, make corrections, and guide them. Visual data, however, has the advantage of being intuitive and natural, and may even be easier to grasp and retain than other forms of information. Take a look at the following activities, many of which will be familiar to you.

Draw concept or relationship maps
These are excellent for making connections between concepts clear and explicit. Nodes on a network represent ideas, and the links between them carry information about their relationship. You can use a concept map to plan a lesson, or recap one that's already happened. Such a map can be used to explain things in the first instance, or you can ask your student to

construct one to show you how much they've retained, as well as any challenging areas. You could create a half-finished map and ask your student to fill in the rest as the lesson progresses—or even ask them to correct mistakes in a deliberately incorrect map.

A good concept map must be functional and logical, however. You need to start with a main concept and add in some sense of hierarchy or structure. Use arrows and boxes to connect concepts, and group related concepts together clearly. Change the arrow style to illustrate different kinds of relationships, for example a darker line to represent a stronger relationship, and move from the general to the specific, the known to the unknown.

Though they can sometimes be confused, mind maps differ from concept maps, and the latter are almost always more organized. A mind map can be used at the beginning of a lesson to gauge current knowledge and reveal everything that is known about a topic. "Brainstorming" is more freeform and gets students to think in creative, open-ended ways, or stimulate discussion. You could spur interest by simply starting with a main topic in the center of the page/board and letting the student elaborate with your guidance.

Use flowcharts and process diagrams

Sometimes, the relationship between different ideas is one of cause and effect, or something that unfolds procedurally in time. Alternatively, a flow chart can represent a decision-making process or conditional logic, i.e. "if X then Y" thinking. These concepts are best illustrated using flowcharts that run in a step-by-step fashion.

Ask students to create a flowchart of a scientific experiment, and outline the processes to be followed under differing outcomes. You can give students a simple flow chart at the start of the lesson that outlines a complex procedure, so they can see where they are in the bigger picture as the lesson progresses. On the other hand, you could teach first and then ask students to compile their own summarizing flowchart. Give them some rules or guidelines for its construction or let them devise their own conventions and symbols.

Get creative with storyboards

Another way to visually present sequential information is through storyboards. A storyboard contains easy to understand comics, visuals or diagrams that simplify the material to highlight its most salient points. Because this can sometimes take time and effort, you might assign a project for your student to create a storyboard themselves, or design a group work project where students must work together to compile something they will all use later as a summary or study aid.

Fishbone diagrams
A fishbone diagram or Ishikawa diagram is a tool for delineating cause and effect relationships, to better understand the factors that went into or could potentially go into bringing about a specific outcome. The head of the "fish" is the problem or effect, and the individual bones drawn toward it are causes grouped into categories.

For example, one category of potential causes of the problem of failing an exam could be "home environment," which you could represent with a diagonal "fishbone." Going further back, you could ask what in turn caused this poor home environment, and list several distractions at home that prevent studying. Even further than that, you could identify the causes for those distractions—family visiting unannounced, or easy access to electronic devices, for example.

Essentially, a fishbone diagram is a directional mind map that seeks to answer the question of *why* something has happened. You can keep asking this question of each individual cause to gain a deeper knowledge of the root causes. Doing an exercise like this trains your student to look at phenomena beyond the superficial symptoms, and go deeper to find the root cause.

These diagrams help students unravel causal relationships. Unlike constructing a logical argument from scratch, they work backwards, almost forensically, to examine a completed situation. You could get students to explore a historical event or a hypothetical situation, or use this method to guide a session of self-reflection or appraisal of performance. You could even reserve this technique for yourself in better understanding your students' position and how they arrived where they are.

Venn diagrams
A picture paints a thousand words; Venn diagrams quickly convey the relationship between two or more topics, and can help students summarize areas of overlap versus areas of difference. You could ask your student to compare and contrast two or three ideas using a Venn diagram, which makes specific

relationships much clearer than if they were written out.

Let's use an example to explore how to use and make Venn diagrams. Let's say you want to classify various animals based on physical traits. In this example, we'll work with three traits, though a Venn diagram can also work with only one point of comparison based on two traits. Our first trait involves animals who can swim. Make a list of all animals that can swim. Some examples are jellyfish, dogs, water moccasins, sea turtles, humans, whales, fish, etc. Now let's consider a second trait, which is animals that can breathe air. As you make this list, you'll notice some examples are in common with the previous trait, swimming. Common examples include humans, dogs, whales, sea turtles, and water moccasins. Other examples of animals that can breathe air, but can't swim, are earthworms and chimpanzees. The third trait we have is legs. Animals that have legs include many that can both swim and breathe air, and some that can only either swim or breathe air. Examples of the former are humans, dogs, etc.

Now, we need to create a diagram based on these similarities. The first step here is to draw a large circle with "Can swim" written on top and write down all the examples in it. Write the animals that can also breathe air on one side, while those that can only swim go on the other. Now, make another circle for animals that "can breathe air" but for this type, make sure the circumference includes animals from your first circle that can swim. So humans, ducks, and dogs will now be a part of both circles, whereas jellyfish will only be in the first circle. Now write all the animals that can only breathe air in the remaining space. Lastly, you have the third circle, "have legs." You need to draw this circle in a way that it includes all animals from the other two circles. So humans, ducks, and dogs, will come in the third circle as well. Animals that are only in the second circle, i.e., chimpanzees, also belong in the third circle.

In the end, you'll have three intersecting circles that visually display which of the three traits each animal has. While the positioning of the names takes some practice, once you get used to it, this can be a powerful visual tool to promote learning.

KWHL chart
Basically:
What do I **k**now?
What do I **w**ant to know?
How can I find out?

What have I learnt?

Get your student to draw up a chart with four columns labelled as above. Now, you can use these four sub-goals to shape an inquiry or learning activity. With a matrix like this outlined beforehand, students can focus their own self-directed projects, and there is a built-in way for them to appraise their own progress and achievement at the end. Again, the inquiry-based approach rears its head; in this instance, a student works to structure their own learning process much as you would as a teacher designing a lesson for them.

For example, your student could be having trouble with a particular accounting/bookkeeping concept. You could set them a KWHL task—can they carefully map out what they already know and don't know? Once they identify the gap in knowledge, their task is to find quality sources of information to fill it. You could use this opportunity to encourage the critical thinking skills already covered, as well as more reflection when the student asks themselves how well their attempt worked. This is effective because they can go back to question 1 and ask again, what do I know? More than before?

What all of these methods have in common is that they:

a. Convey a lot of data or information in a quick, concise way
b. Highlight relationships, causal connections, similarities and differences, or sequences between data points—i.e. they are about connections
c. Allow you to organize material so you can gauge understanding, offer feedback, correct or expand on relevant areas

As always, teaching techniques (whether based on group activities or visual aids) need to be applied *after* you've gained a clear understanding of where your student is and where you want to take them with your lesson. The better you understand the nature of what you're trying to teach, the more you are able to choose appropriate techniques that will actually do what they're meant to.

If you want students to gain an in-depth understanding of a complex procedure, you could ask them to observe a role play of that procedure going wrong and take notes, which they then use to construct a fishbone diagram. If you want your student to gain a rich understanding of the current theory on a certain topic, you could ask them to closely read and annotate a text and summarize its material.

Another student could do the same with a different text and when they meet to discuss, the students could work together to create a Venn diagram summarizing the key points of similarity between the texts. Taking it even further, you could then get them to work alone and compile an essay expanding on these similarities, where they can synthesize a completely new analysis and offer their own response.

As you can see, the only limit is your imagination, and techniques and methods can be combined or adapted to suit your needs, and your students. Get students to engage in debate with one another or you, and simultaneously put together a flowchart for the debate process. At the end of the lesson assign a "mini-quiz" with KWHL elements. Can the student reflect on their progress and make suggestions for what to include in the next lesson?

Takeaways

- Once you've mastered the more straightforward teaching techniques, you might like to try more advanced methods. PBL or problem-based learning, for example, is an integrative approach where students are presented with a problem and guided to find the solution for themselves, gaining deeper understanding. PBL is excellent for giving students responsibility for their own learning, and creates realistic, applicable and memorable lessons.
- The Socratic method is another depth approach that rests on strategic inquiry. Questions can be used to unearth assumptions and bias, to probe for richer understanding, to flesh out perspectives, explore consequences and implications, examine an argument's deeper rationale, or even look more closely at the question itself.
- The key to the Socratic approach is asking questions so that your interlocutor or student has enough room to express their opinion. Once you've got them to reveal what they think, probe them further by either asking for clarifications, elaborating on something they glossed over, or problematizing something they said. These tactics force students to learn and understand new concepts by having gaps in their knowledge exposed.

- Critical thinking is a great approach for more advanced concepts, as it encourages meta-cognition about both the quality of one's thoughts and the material and learning process itself. Critical thinking is characterized by an attitude of open-mindedness, and a tolerance for ambiguity or uncertainty that takes nothing for granted. Often, it involves following an inquiry-based approach wherein you're continuously asking your students questions that challenge their beliefs in ways that stimulate discussion and learning.

- Other advanced techniques can use group work to aid learning (for example student-teacher tasks, "pair and share," debate or student observation) or relevant visual materials (such as relationship maps, flowcharts, Venn diagrams or storyboards).

- All these more advanced techniques require the student to be proactive in their learning, and they allow the teacher to not only gauge understanding but offer useful feedback.

Chapter 5. The Student Environment

In the previous chapters, our focus has been on what you as the prospective teacher can do to make your student's learning experience as good as it can be. But throughout, we've acknowledged that a teacher's role is always that of a *facilitator*—someone who allows the natural processes of learning to occur optimally. A big part of this is creating the environmental conditions most conducive to genuine learning.

The student environment is more than just the immediate physical surroundings, though. Here, we'll discuss how the student, teacher, environment and material are all in close relationship, and an effective teacher is one who can make sure all four are properly aligned to best lead to success. This requires a set of effective attitudes, an understanding of habit and motivation, and a spirit of resilience, as well as a learning atmosphere that fosters learning rather than fear or avoidance.

Teachers can often have difficulty not with the material itself or finding the smartest, most efficient way to present it—rather, their trouble comes in when they try to inspire and motivate students who simply don't care! It's as though in teaching, there are always two lessons running in parallel—one concerning the actual material at hand, and another running in the background, where the student is learning discipline, stamina and self-regulation as they move through the process of learning.

Understanding Motivation

Unless a student is motivated to learn, they won't learn. Without motivation, intelligence doesn't matter, and the supposed value of the material doesn't matter either. But why are people motivated to do some things and not others?

A very simple theory to explain human motivation is called expectancy theory, and it basically states that people act in accordance with what outcomes they *expect* to happen following that action. The theory states that, even if you're unaware of it, you will:

a. Assess the likelihood that an amount of effort spent will lead to a predictable outcome or change in performance (how hard do I have to work?)
b. Assess the extent to which any effort is directly linked to a desired outcome (what will that work get me?) and
c. Decide how appealing that outcome is to you personally, according to your needs and values (how valuable is this outcome to me?)

So, your old PE teacher might have wanted to teach you the rules of some sport you didn't really like, but if you knew that they would probably grade you well no matter what, you were likely far less motivated to make an effort. Similarly, if you knew that your PE grade factored only minimally into your total yearly performance at school anyway, you might find it hard to be motivated, since doing well in PE wasn't directly related to a goal you did care about—passing the year. Finally, you might simply decide that PE just didn't matter that much to you, given your overall life goals and values.

How hard your students are willing to work depends heavily on how hard they *need* to work to achieve success, how likely it is this work will be rewarded, and whether the reward is something that is truly perceived as valuable. Effort is always linked to performance and to reward, and so, when we teach, we need to be aware of the links our students are making for themselves. Unless all these are aligned, it's unlikely someone will feel motivated to act for very long.

Importantly, there is no universally appealing outcome or goal—rather, it's what a person individually *perceives* as valuable. You might believe that the topic you're teaching is immensely valuable and can't understand why others aren't as motivated to understand it as you are—but that's because they've made different assessments when weighing up effort and likely reward.

You can see where this is going: to inspire our students, we need to work with their intrinsic motivations. It makes complete sense—why on earth would you be motivated to do something that has an unpredictable relationship to any outcome, or toward an outcome we don't particularly want? Another key point here is that motivation is something that's powered by our perception and appraisal of the *future*—it's in what we expect and anticipate.

This means that even if a particular action really is in someone's best interests, they may still fail to find motivation if they have no idea what to expect from you or the material in front of them. This bears repeating: the reality of the situation is irrelevant—what makes the difference is your student's perceptions. If you're lucky, you have a student who is already sufficiently motivated to seek out study, but even if this is the case, you may still need to understand and kindle their motivation during those times when it's knocked down by challenges, setbacks or feelings of being stalled.

A great way to motivate students is obvious when you think about it: increase the perceived value of the material. How you do this is up to you, but think of ways to first understand your student's values and principles, then connect those to the material. For example, you may not care much about learning about web design, but since you do care about staying competitive in your industry and saving money and time by not hiring others to fix bugs on your business website, you might feel more motivated to learn a little about web design.

Try to see things from your student's perspective. Can you design tasks that don't feel like phony hypotheticals or irrelevant scenarios? Make tasks as authentic and hands-on as possible, so your student really witnesses the real-world value of the skills and knowledge they're acquiring. Almost all skills are transferrable—find ways to express the usefulness of what you're teaching (according to their estimations, not yours!).

Even things that are perceived as valuable need a little help now and then, so build in regular rewards to make the effort worth everyone's while. Praise and feedback are invaluable—can you stop now and then to acknowledge the progress made, and give everyone a pat on the back? Encourage your students to not only appraise their outcomes but feel proud of their achievements. If you can show some enthusiasm for this process yourself (*genuine* enthusiasm, of course), some of it will likely rub off.

Your strategy is to build expectation of a positive outcome—it's this expectation that inspires students to keep working even through difficult or boring patches. Make sure that you are crystal clear about what they can expect in future—what are the goals, why are you aiming toward those goals, and how will you both measure success when you've achieved them? Keep track of the level of challenge, and make sure that it's not too difficult, not too easy, but in the sweet spot in between where overcoming challenge genuinely feels like an achievement.

It's also important that students perceive the process as being fair. Nothing kills motivation more than knowing that the rules are inconsistent, or that some will be favored for seemingly no good reason. After all, why work hard if the results are not guaranteed—or even if hard work is punished? You want your students to know that there is a direct, predictable and quantifiable relationship between what they put in and what they get out. With your feedback, they need to know exactly why they succeed and why they fail; being confused about the effect of their efforts is likely to sap any enthusiasm.

The Trick of Gamification

If there's anyone who knows something about kindling motivation, it's the gaming industry. In fact, many would argue that game developers and marketers are so good at capturing and maintaining attention that it borders on manufacturing addiction. Wouldn't it be great if you could study and learn with the same intense focus and engagement as you felt for an addictive video game? Well, this is more or less the theory behind gamification, or the use of video game principles and elements in a non-gaming context.

Every parent has noticed that motivation, sustained attention and hard work are easy to muster so long as their child really cares about the "game" in front of them. But learning is a game too, or at least it can be made into one. The principle is really obvious—if you make learning fun, then your student will naturally want to do more of it; no force or self-discipline required. Have you ever seen a kitten play? That kitten is simultaneously learning the complicated motor skills needed to hunt while also having the time of its life!

Everyone instinctively knows what counts as fun and play, and what counts as the serious (and boring) business of learning. But what precise part of the game experience can be introduced into the learning environment to "gamify" it? If you've played a single video game in your life, you probably know some of these elements already.

Firstly, a fundamental game element is the concept of **step-wise progress**. In games, you move through levels, or earn points, or beat out competitors. There's a sense of direction and building purpose, perhaps even competition, and the student always knows that this progress is important; they know how progress is defined and they understand the steps needed to make that progress.

To help with tracking progress in learning, you can use online tools like Moodle, Canvas, Piazza, and others. Such websites allow you to post all your modules and assignments, showing students what percentage of them have been covered in class already. Students can be asked to submit their assignments, access readings, view grades, and even ask questions through such platforms. This engenders a sense of progress, since that number on total progress goes up frequently.

Secondly, a game may often contain some kind of **narrative** which may include characters— again, the idea is that there is a fixed field through which the student moves, be it a map, board, or chronological story they work through. Alternatively, you can present your course as one long story. So, if you're teaching the history of the American Revolution, you need not teach it as merely a series of events. Involve different perspectives and theories on the start and course of the Revolution, how it was perceived then and now, include interesting anecdotes, etc. What's more, **scaffolding** is natural, as players move through increasing levels of challenge and complexity. This means there's always an opportunity on the horizon to "level up," with clear and obvious gains in mastery as you go (for example, with the winning of badges or the unlocking of new tools and skills).

A key feature of games is that the **game-player is in control** of play. They don't design the game world or set up its rules, but they are empowered to make decisions and watch the outcome unfold. They are in charge and can steer the experience, and, if the stakes are high enough, this provides both a sense of challenge and achievement when those challenges are completed. A big appeal of games is that the effect of any one choice is usually immediate, i.e. **instant feedback**. The player almost always gets to see the result or outcome of their choices at once, and can adapt and learn in real time. This makes their actions feel relevant and engaging, since a clear and direct link between action and consequence is established.

Many games also contain a **collaborative** element, and require teamwork and strategic communication to solve a bigger problem as a group. The feeling of social connection and shared fun can naturally make the topic at hand feel more relevant and meaningful.

So, how can we build these concepts into our lessons, making them more enjoyable and engaging? In a broad sense, gamification can take two paths: you could alter the actual content being taught, or you could alter the mechanism or structure through which that content is being presented. For example, you might be trying to teach your student some new vocabulary in a language they're learning. You could gamify your approach by sorting different words into levels and using flashcards that prompt the student to recall definitions. If they do so, and beat the difficult "boss" word, they go to the next level.

That would be an example of gamifying the structure—the vocabulary content stays much the same. But you could get more creative and introduce themes and ideas that go beyond the plain content. You could, for example, position yourself and the student as two opposing players that must try to outwit one another, with you posing words and them defending the "attack" with an accurate definition in English. They may win "XP" by doing this or get to advance on a board with an avatar or counter. But as you can see, there's nothing intrinsically battle-like about vocabulary—this is content that you are introducing to make existing content easier to engage with.

As you can see, gamification is actually a perfect approach to take advantage of what intrinsically motivates people—we can all be productive and challenge ourselves, so long as the process is perceived as enjoyable and meaningful. Gamifying your approach to teaching doesn't just inspire your student to pay more attention and actually retain what they learn; it also makes the entire exercise more psychologically satisfying. How freeing to realize that learning doesn't have to be serious and dull to be effective!

With a game-like approach to tackling new knowledge and skills, students are set up as active agents directing their own learning—something you'll recognize from the five pedagogical approaches. With the student centered and owning their progress, they can essentially play in a realm where they try out different things and adapt as they go, without fear of failing or serious consequence. As a teacher you yourself can incorporate some of this philosophy when you piece together an approach or lesson plan for your student. Ask yourself, how can you continually meet your student where they are, and challenge them afresh as learning progresses?

An educational game is a little like a simpler, safer version of real life, where we get to try on the mindset of an explorer applying the scientific method to reality. How does this work? Why? What do I have to do? How can I get from A to B, and what are the rules limiting my actions? Recall the bases of motivation we discussed earlier:

a. Assess the likelihood that an amount of effort spent will lead to a predictable outcome or change in performance (how hard do I have to work?)
b. Assess the extent to which any effort is directly linked to a desired outcome (what will that work get me?) and
c. Decide how appealing that outcome is to you personally, according to your needs and values (how valuable is this outcome to me?)

It's easy to see how a gamified approach ticks all these boxes, and not only motivates students but improves their enjoyment of the process, as they learn. Rather than dead content being passively handed over for the student to absorb, it becomes a kind of "Player Two" that can dynamically respond and interact to the student as they learn. Far more fun!

As a teacher, when you attempt to gamify a lesson, you need to nevertheless keep your goal and approach firmly in mind—not all play is useful or leads to learning. As you plan a task, ask yourself:

- Have you set up a step-like sequence of tasks that increase in challenge incrementally?
- Have you just spelled things out for your student, or have you left it to them to discover the game mechanisms for themselves (far more interesting!)?
- Does your game contain immediate feedback that allows the student to alter their behavior and quickly try again?
- Is your game free from "seriousness," i.e. is it really safe to try out a few things without penalty?
- Have you made it very clear how your student can level up, and is the challenge appropriate to their ability?

- Have you clearly outlined the goal, purpose and rules of the game, i.e. set up clear parameters for what the student can and can't control?

Watch your student closely as they do a task to see if they're frustrated or engaged. If you see them advancing too quickly, ramp up the challenge to stop them from getting bored. Pace things and mix them up just as your student is getting too familiar. Before you know it, they're in the "flow" of the game and learning, and hours can pass this way with seemingly no effort spent.

Even if you're struggling to see how to teach your specific subject and specific student using game principles, you can always change up your language to great effect. For example, you don't do worksheets and exercises but embark on quests or complete missions. You don't get grades but XP, rankings or the opportunity to unlock hidden levels. Rather than doing group work you are organized into guilds, and so on.

A word about extrinsic motivation

Some teachers are critical of gamification in the classroom, believing not only that it might not always work, but also that it creates entirely the wrong mindset, i.e. focuses on extrinsic rather than intrinsic motivation. You might have wondered this yourself when reading about rewards and the use of expectation in boosting motivation. If you're just encouraging someone to act because of the perceived incentives attached to doing so, have you really created any real, lasting change? Is this really the smartest way to engage students?

The difference between intrinsic and extrinsic motivation is simple: when we are intrinsically motivated, we act because of forces driving us from within our own perceptions, attitudes or beliefs; when motivated externally, we act because of some external force, such as reward or punishment. It's the difference between doing something for its own sake, and doing a thing specifically so that you can gain access to something else.

The trouble is, if you remove game dynamics like competition or arbitrary challenge, is there anything left to motivate the student to carry on? There's no doubt about it: gamification is a reward-based system that relies completely on extrinsic motivation, and for that reason, it may not always be appropriate, or as effective as encouraging students to independently find their own genuine, internal appraisal of value for the task at hand. Some knowledge is not valuable for any extrinsic purpose, but merely for its own sake. Knowledge isn't power because it helps you achieve certain outcomes, but because it ensures that you become an informed individual who knows things others might ignore due to the perceived lack of value.

If you want to merely get the student engaged and paying attention, there's nothing better than gamification. On the other hand, if you want to kindle a genuine love for the subject that persists after the game gimmicks are removed, gamification may not be enough. The ideal scenario is a student who is independently and genuinely interested in the material. But for this to happen, they need to feel that their success in under their control, that they have the necessary skills, and that their goal is worth attaining in the first place (i.e. the motivational conditions we outlined earlier).

Things get a little more complex when we consider that not everyone will respond to gamified material in quite the same way. A classic "player" might happily slot into the competitive aspect, being motivated by the rewards and desire to win. A "socializer" may get more value from the relational and cooperative aspects of play. An "achiever" almost doesn't care about the mechanisms; they have their eye on the prize and want to win it. Finally, the "philanthropist" might care more about overall meaning and value in the game, whether they win or lose.

In other words, gamifying your lesson is not a substitute for understanding your student's unique personality and preferences. There are some students who may even respond negatively to gamification. The "overjustification" effect of rewarding certain behavior can immediately make that behavior seem less desirable, and such a student may actually perform better in the absence of pressure, competition or an external incentive.

It's your job as a teacher to closely examine how your student experiences reward-based systems. You need to really know *why* they are doing some things, and not others, and furthermore you need to understand the deeper source of their motivation. You don't want to introduce a system that actually detracts from your student's natural motivation and interest, or offer some reward that means nothing to them. Even students who find gamified activities appealing will tire of them eventually, looking for something a little more meaningful. Like any addiction, the user can acquire tolerance and need a greater and greater promise of reward to carry out the same behavior!

Watch carefully to see your students' energy and interest levels, and note the actual effect that rewards have on their performance. They may start to just tick the boxes, going for the reward rather than focusing on how best to do the task at hand. For example, if you see your student rushing through an exercise just to win the points attached to its completion, without taking time to complete the exercise with care, then gamification might not be working. Unfortunately, there is no replacement for occasional diligence and effort.

As with any other teaching technique, the question of whether to gamify or not comes down to one thing: does it work in this particular instance, or is it ultimately ineffective? On this note, let's turn to another aspect of the broader academic "environment" that has significant consequences for how well your student performs.

Academic Buoyancy

The concept of *academic buoyancy* is the second key to overcoming our own internal obstacles to learning.

Learning is bound to be difficult, even for those with supposed innate intelligence. Nothing comes easy, at least not at the levels of mastery we are aiming for. And yet, so many people take themselves out of the running by giving up at the first sign of hardship.

People who *don't* give up when they're faced with learning challenges are said to have *academic buoyancy*. Like intelligence, this isn't an inborn characteristic that some are born with, but rather a set of skills that can be learned and habits that can be cultivated to result in the ability to push past challenges and keep learning.

Confidence is just one element of academic buoyancy, but confidence alone is what allows us to overcome our fears and anxieties. In the first chapter, we discussed how confidence can unlock your lack of motivation. Imagine how much more empowered you would feel with the hardships of learning if you could embody every element.

Researchers from the University of Sydney and the University of Oxford have identified five Cs that, if developed, will result in academic buoyancy. These five Cs are *composure, confidence, coordination, commitment, and control*. They are not specific to learning, but they are traits that certainly improve it.

It will be apparent why these qualities are important to overcoming obstacles associated with learning—most of them are truly not about the content or information itself. Rather, most obstacles have to do with our mindset; our belief and sense of perseverance ends up being what separates most effective learners at the end of the day. Their influence is far, far greater than any of the techniques in this book. Is this to say that where there is a will, there is a way? Yes—learning in large part depends on how you feel about it, and the rest is just about saving time and working smarter.

Composure is the ability to manage and minimize anxiety. When learners feel anxious while engaging in their studies, it's usually because they're afraid of being ashamed and embarrassed. What if people find out we're trying to learn something, and expect us to display our knowledge? What if we fail completely when this happens? *What if we fail?* The fear can be paralyzing.

When people can't manage their anxiety, they are weighed down by their fear and crippled by the tension it produces in their bodies. In the worst cases, worries overcome the thoughts of the learner, preventing the student from focusing on and understanding new information. But there's good news: those fears are entirely baseless.

As anxiety is largely based on the fear of failure, we must directly address that. When we think about fear, we think about the worst-case scenario. Whatever we "fail" at, we imagine the world ending as a direct result. This is known as catastrophization, and it occurs whenever you ignore the realistic consequences and jump to drastic conclusions.

This tendency is conquered by managing your self-talk. Acknowledge that negative things may happen, but that many of your thoughts may be irrational and fictitious. Consider the alternative explanations and outcomes.

If you find yourself worrying, counter that worry with optimism. If you berate yourself for a mistake, remind yourself that it's a learning opportunity and that you'll do better next time. Any negative thought can be successfully and honestly countered by positive, encouraging, forgiving, and accepting alternatives. With time, the brain comes to accept these retorts as more valid than the negative, fearful thoughts. If anxiety is a problem for you, be persistent. This bugaboo really can be beaten. You can gain the composure you need to be academically buoyant.

Confidence, also called self-efficacy, is the belief that you are able to perform a specific task. When we lack confidence, we are certain we can't successfully accomplish a goal. We talk ourselves down, insult ourselves, and belittle any progress we make. When this happens, we often give up on our goal early before we can prove to ourselves and others that we're a failure. The trouble is that giving up is failing too; it can be satisfying to confirm these negative beliefs about ourselves, but it's far more satisfying—and less stressful—to set our doubts aside and actually reach our goals.

If you're ready to improve your confidence, there are two main techniques to employ. The first, as we saw in the section on composure, is self-talk. When your brain tells you that you're a failure or that a subject is too hard for you to learn, counter that thought with an assertion that you're going to keep studying, and with time and effort, you will succeed. If you keep questioning these thoughts, they really will fade in time.

The second method is more concrete: goal-setting. We gain confidence naturally when we accomplish tasks. When we have a track record of success, it becomes harder and harder to believe our doubts have any credibility. The fastest way to do this is to create daily, or even hourly, study goals, and to watch yourself meet them over and over again. When this happens, congratulate yourself! Each goal you reach gets you one step closer to your ultimate goal of skill mastery. More than that, each goal you reach demonstrates that you have the skill and fortitude to reach the targets you set for yourself. It's a sign that your confidence is real and legitimate.

Coordination is your ability to plan and manage your time effectively. When people fail to do this, they often fall prey to *The Planning Fallacy*. This fallacy points out that people are poor at determining how long tasks take to complete. As a general rule, we presume tasks will take less time than they actually need. Worse, when we presume things won't take very long, we often put those tasks off, because we feel like we have plenty of time to get them done. This is usually untrue, and then we find ourselves with late assignments and failed work tasks.

Several steps can be taken to eliminate this problem. Minimizing distractions in your work area is a great way to start. Turn off your phone, close your door, and tell friends or family that you're busy and not to be disturbed. You should invariably do this soon after you gain a new task to complete or subject to study. Putting things off leads to being late, while doing them immediately takes advantage of all the time you have. Lastly, it's best to do the longest, most difficult task first. Leaving it for last will produce a false sense of security and may lead to your work being incomplete at the time it's due. Getting it out of the way does the opposite, setting you up for easier tasks and an early finish.

Commitment, also called grit, is a combination of passion and persistence that can be nurtured to help you reach your goals. It's easy to study for a day or a week, but attempts to build new habits often fail. We find ourselves listlessly settling into the couch to watch another movie or television show, without putting any more effort into bettering ourselves. This keeps us in the same life situation, wasting precious time, when we could be using those same hours to improve ourselves and our circumstances.

As in the previous two categories, self-talk can be a useful tool in bolstering commitment. Talking yourself into doing things and ensuring yourself that you can make it to the end are useful tools. Having others support you in a similar way and encourage you to study when you're flagging can bolster your sense of personal responsibility and keep you trucking along even when your energy is waning.

Finally, understanding what you are sacrificing and committing for can be powerful. Without a sense of how we stand to benefit, or what pain we will clearly avoid, we can sometimes lose motivation. What dreams does this information help you attain? What hardships and difficulties will be removed once you master this information? Keep these in mind and know that you are working for something greater than the current moment of discomfort.

Finally, *control*. We have to feel like we can control our fates. There are multiple aspects of this. First, we should feel that we have the ability and capacity to achieve the learning outcomes we want. Lacking this makes us feel like we are in motion just for motion's sake, never getting closer to the end goal. We covered this in an earlier chapter, but there is no real thing as innate intelligence. Well, there is, but it doesn't really affect ninety-nine percent of us in the middle of the bell curve. Understand that with hard work, the result you want is possible, and that struggles are an unavoidable part of the process. Discomfort should be the expectation, not the exception.

Second, we should feel a sense of ownership over our learning process. When we have a sense of control in our work, we feel personal responsibility, or a sense of ownership, that propels us to do our best and keep working in the face of setbacks. When we don't have that, working and studying can seem futile, like a waste of time. We will simply feel that we are being told what to do, and this is adding insult to injury.

This can be addressed by proactively making sure of what your goals are and tailoring your everyday work to reach them. Take your fate into your own hands and create your own plan. You always have the choice to float toward other people's expectations, goals, and plans, or create a personalized set for yourself to follow.

Learning in itself is not a difficult task. But missing any of these academic buoyancy elements will simply set you up for failure. They are more prerequisites to effective learning than tactics in themselves.

Academic buoyancy is perhaps better framed as *resilience*: the ability to adapt to stressful situations. More resilient people are able to "roll with the punches" and adapt to adversity without lasting difficulties; less resilient people have a harder time with stress and life changes, both major and minor. It's been found that those who deal with minor stresses more easily can also manage major crises with greater ease, so resilience has its benefits for daily life as well as for the rare major catastrophe.

Psychologist Susan Kobasa noted three elements to resilience: (1) looking at difficulties as a challenge, (2) committing to achieving a goal no matter what, and (3) limiting their efforts and even concerns only to factors that they have control over.

Another psychologist named Martin Seligman noted three different elements of resilience: (1) seeing negative events as temporary and limited, (2) not letting negative events define them or their perspective, and (3) not overly blaming or denigrating themselves for negative events. His general theme appears to be letting negativity pass as temporary and not indicative of personal shortcomings.

It's clear how any of those six resilience factors can play a role in achieving the learning goals we want. It's simply about how you bounce back from failure. Failure is a part of life, and it's what we do after the fact that determines our character and, ultimately, our success.

Productive Failure

In most situations, we tie accomplishment with success: winning, positive outcomes, and finding solutions. But in learning, a key component in achievement is *failing*.

Productive failure is an idea identified by Manu Kapur, a researcher at the National Institute of Education in Singapore. The philosophy builds on the learning paradox, wherein *not* arriving at the desired effect is as valuable as prevailing, if not more. This is not the emotional impact, but rather, the neurological impact.

Kapur stated that the accepted model of instilling knowledge—giving students structure and guidance early and continuing support until the students can get it on their own—might not be the best way to actually promote learning. Although that model intuitively makes sense, according to Kapur, it's best to let students flounder by themselves without outside help.

Kapur conducted a trial with two groups of students. In one group, students were given a set of problems with full instructional support from teachers on-site. The second group was given the same problems but received no teacher help whatsoever. Instead, the second group of students had to collaborate to find the solutions.

The supported group was able to solve the problems correctly, while the group left to itself was not. But without instructional support, this second group was forced to do deeper dives into the problems by working together. They generated ideas about the nature of the problems and speculated on what potential solutions might look like. They tried to understand the root of the problems and what methods were available to solve them. Multiple solutions, approaches, and angles were investigated that ended up providing a three-dimensional understanding of the problems.

The two groups were then tested on what they had just learned, and the results weren't even close. The group without teacher assistance *significantly outperformed* the other group. The group that did not solve the problems discovered what Kapur deemed a "hidden efficacy" in failure: they nurtured a deeper understanding of the structure of the problems through group investigation and process.

The second group may not have solved the problem itself, but they learned more about the aspects of the problem. Going forward, when those students encountered a new problem on another test, they were able to use the knowledge they generated through their trial more effectively than the passive recipients of an instructor's expertise.

Consequently, Kapur asserted that the important parts of the second group's process were their miscues, mistakes, and fumbling. When that group made the active effort to learn by themselves, they retained more knowledge needed for future problems.

Three conditions, Kapur said, make productive failure an effective process:

- Choose problems that "challenge but do not frustrate."

- Give learners the chance to explain and elaborate their processes.

- Allow learners to compare and contrast good and bad solutions.

Struggling with something is a positive condition to learning, though it requires discipline and a sense of delayed gratification. This runs counter to our instincts. How can we, so to speak, let failing work for us?

Chances are you'll come across a moment or two of defeat in your process, along with the temptation to give up. You may even sense this before you start, which can lead to crippling anxiety that can hover over your work.

Expect but don't succumb to frustration.

Anticipating frustration in advance is just good planning—but you also have to plan for how to deal with it. Sketch out a plan or idea on how to alleviate frustration when it happens—most often, this will be taking a break from the situation to recharge and getting some momentary distance from the problem. Quite often, the mere act of pausing allows for objectivity to seep in, letting you see the hang-up more clearly. But in any case, it will abate the most immediate anxieties you're feeling and give you the chance to approach the issue from a more relaxed frame of mind.

It's a matter of being comfortable with a state of mental discomfort and confusion. This can be akin to juggling ten balls in the air at once and not being sure when you can place them down.

Learning mode is different from results mode, and they have entirely different measures of success. When you want to learn, you are just looking for an increase in knowledge—*any* increase is successful learning. Reframe your expectations to make the learning as important as the result—*more* important, if possible.

Explicit and static knowledge, such as facts and dates, doesn't necessarily benefit from this. It doesn't need to. But transmitting deep and layered comprehension cannot just be plugged into the brain. It must be manipulated and applied, and failure is inherent in that process. In a way, failures function similarly to the types of questions we discussed in an earlier chapter, where they slowly allow you to triangulate knowledge and understanding based on what's *not* working and what's *not* true.

In the end, failure acts as a blueprint for our next steps. It is a test run that didn't go as planned and thus allows you to rectify pinpointed matters for the future.

For example, let's say you're planting a vegetable garden, noting the steps and techniques you use along the way, and when it's time to harvest, some of your plants don't come out the way they are supposed to. Is it because you used the wrong soil? Use your resources to find out *why* that soil was wrong and what it needs to look like. Was the failed plant too close to another? Learn techniques for maximizing placement within a small space.

Hidden in all of this is the fact that living and acting to avoid failure, even just in learning, leads to very different results than someone who actively seeks success. One approach wants to limit exposure and risk, while the other is focused on the end goal no matter the cost. Failure doesn't have to be your friend, but it *will* be your occasional companion, like it or not. With that in mind, it probably makes more sense to embody the approach that is about taking more risk—and also reaping greater rewards.

Freedom from Judgment

In a way, one of the best lessons any teacher can impart on any student is a healthy attitude toward risk and failure. The mindset with which we as teachers approach the entire learning process communicates powerfully to our students what the parameters of learning are, its values, and so on. And so if we talk about failure and how it can actually teach us more effectively than success, we also need to talk about the *psychological* aspects of failure when learning is concerned.

A learning environment free from judgment is one that fosters a robust attitude toward failure or defeat. If failure is so important to the learning process, we need to make sure our students feel free enough to take risks and try new things without feeling stupid for doing so. Judgment is an ego game—it's part of the "fixed mindset" that sees knowledge and learning as something to bolster one's personal identity, or win an argument.

The trouble is when the ego makes self-worth and identity dependent on success. The other side of this is that we then experience failure, mistakes, ignorance, delay or defeat as an attack to our very identity, and a threat to our self-worth. So, instead of thinking, "I failed," we think, "*I'm* a failure." You can see which attitude is most likely to lead to self-correction and learning. The irony is that clinging to the idea of being right and never making a mistake or failing makes us *less* resilient to adversity, and less likely to truly evolve and learn.

It's a paradox; when we embark on learning we obviously want to gain more mastery, insight and understanding. But the price for this is often the experience of being a beginner, who must constantly face their own ignorance and lack of skill. This is why it's important to appreciate the meta-skill of being able to tolerate not only failure, but uncertainty, ambiguity and complexity. A good teacher makes their student feel like they can experiment, try things, fail, adjust, and ask questions safely and without any consequences for their sense of self-worth or identity.

But you might be wondering—does learning really have to be such a grueling and mistake-ridden experience? Surely positive feelings of success and pride are also great motivators? You can imagine that routinely having to face your own shortcomings or defeats would quickly become demoralizing and lead to less learning, not more. To understand this balance better, we can turn to the concept of the Losada Ratio, first introduced by psychologists Marcial Losada and Barbara Frederickson.

The idea is that there is a fixed ratio of negative emotions to positive ones that would best support a successful, balanced life. Using mathematical models, the pair found the ideal ratio to fall between around three and eleven, meaning that the number of positive comments, ideas, thoughts, feelings etc. needed to be around three to eleven times greater than negative ones, in order for a person to thrive optimally.

Positive feedback, reward and reinforcement helps. But too much can have the opposite effect.

Criticism, failure and defat can also support learning. But too much can demotivate and frustrate. However, if people experience roughly three times as much positive information as negative, they will flourish. At ratios above 11:1, however, the performance gains are lost, i.e. the "Losada Line" is reached—at least according to this theory.

As it happens, the original Losada Ratio paper has now been seriously criticized for lacking scientific validity and the concept has been outright debunked. Nevertheless, its popularity does suggest that there is some value in the idea that positive and negative emotional experiences ought to be in optimal balance.

As teachers, we can dismiss the specific science behind the theory while still appreciating that our students likely do have an ideal ratio between challenge and ease, achievement and disappointment. Again, there is no substitution for working dynamically with the unique student in front of you. It may be that the positive:negative ratio changes daily or depends on the subject at hand, but it's probably true that most of us work best when the positive outweighs the negative.

Understanding Feedback

Whenever we engage with the environment or some new piece of information, we get feedback. Feedback is simply cause and effect, and lets us know the outcome of our actions. As a teacher, however, you facilitate this process and give your student feedback that is deliberately intended to support, guide and encourage them. Feedback is information on how we are doing relative to our goal. It's like a conversation—it's in the back and forth that meaning emerges. It's simple: when a student knows what effect their actions are having overall, they can adjust themselves, ultimately improving their performance, self-evaluation and awareness.

Somewhere along the line, it became common to blandly throw a "great job!" at students, regardless of their performance. Empty or insincere praise is as useless, however, as handing out a grade with no elaboration on how it was determined. Giving good, actionable and meaningful feedback as a teacher is an art. It's all about *how* feedback is given, rather than the specific words or phrases. We've already seen that on balance feedback should probably be more in favor of the positive than the negative, but there are other characteristics of quality feedback.

- **Respect**. As a baseline, students should feel that they are treated with dignity and politeness, no matter who they are. This allows feedback to be received for what it is, rather than as an attack on the individual. For example, in a male-dominated workplace, feedback for a female employee will likely only be effective if she genuinely feels as though what she is told is really about her performance, and not the fact that she is female.

- **Timeliness**. Feedback should be given as close as possible to the event it relates to. For example, don't wait for two weeks to evaluate performance on a project; your feedback is unlikely to "stick." On that note, for feedback to be formative, it needs to be provided often and in small doses—a single big evaluation can leave students feeling in the dark in the meantime, and can give avoidable errors a chance to compound.

- **Be specific.** You want your student to know exactly where they stand, and why. Vague feedback can feel stressful and leave people feeling bad about themselves. Instead, be clear about exactly what the student is doing right, what needs improvement, how they're performing against others or a fixed standard and, most importantly, the concrete steps they can take to remedy the situation. If a student simply feels they've been insulted or put down, they won't have any idea on what to do next, or how to improve.

- **Use the "sandwich" method.** A useful structure to follow is to begin with a compliment, move onto the correction, then end with a compliment. This way the feedback is cushioned in a context of positivity more likely to inspire and encourage. For example, "Your opening was great, and you have excellent breath control. The high notes are still feeling a little unsteady, but you finished strong, particularly that last chorus." Naturally, the compliments have to be sincere!

- **Describe rather than evaluate**. "Showing your work here has made it so much easier to follow your process" is more effective feedback than, "Hey, nice job showing your work." The difference is subtle, but the first encourages internal motivation and explains *why* something is being perceived favorably. The student can come to their own conclusions, and feel a more genuine pride than if they had merely been told "you're great!" Similarly, focus feedback on actions, skills or abilities, rather than personal attributes. This encourages a growth mindset that increases tolerance for failure and mistakes. So, saying "the follow-through on your backstroke is really getting stronger" is actually more likely to instill confidence than "you're a naturally gifted swimmer," which doesn't give the student much to work with. Avoid advice ("you should do XYZ") for the same reason.

- **Don't make it personal**. If a student is particularly sensitive, you can find ways to offer feedback without even referring to them directly. Model incorrect performance and then critique yourself, or talk about a hypothetical example. Depending on your students' personalities, it may also work to ask them to evaluate themselves, or even give you feedback on your teaching—this makes the learning process feel like a mutual collaboration rather than a power dynamic with the teacher evaluating the student. For the same reason, avoid feedback explaining how pleased or upset you personally are by your student's performance—it's not about you!

- **Mix it up**. You can give feedback in a variety of ways. Pay attention to what works for your student and tailor your communication so it has the best chance of being heard. Consider again your student's innate motivators and appeal to those when giving feedback; for example, you may emphasize the relative ranking of a performance if you know your student is motivated by mastery and winning. Try giving feedback verbally, but also leave notes, or small, unobtrusive written corrections. Sometimes, a simple smile or thumbs up does the job. You could even get feedback from a third party that you look at together with your student.

Even if you're friendly, reasonable and transparent in your feedback, try to remember that criticism can *still* be difficult to stomach, so be kind. Try to strike a balance between sincerity and compassion, and avoid overwhelming your student by dumping lots of information on them all at once.

Giving feedback is about making realistic adjustments to learning, but it's also an emotional experience, so be mindful of this and give your student space to process what you've told them in their own way. If you never deliver feedback with an air of judgment, your student will quickly learn not to take it that way. One method for encouraging this neutral mindset is to put the feedback to use. Good feedback should be **actionable**. Ask your student to tell you how they plan to or have already incorporated your suggestions. This is empowering and can focus the mind, allowing the student to quickly move on from any potential feelings of embarrassment or disappointment.

Even better, when you link feedback to meaningful action, you get to see trends unfolding—the next time you evaluate your student, you could give them what might be the most satisfying piece of feedback of all: "I can see that you took that feedback from before and really ran with it, and because of your hard work you've definitely improved. Well done."

For every piece of feedback you give, try to build in an opportunity to respond to that feedback and actually make meaningful changes.

Good feedback has a way of helping the student internalize their own ability to self-evaluate and adjust after observation. It teaches them how to think of their own progress. No matter what feedback you give or when, positive language can be extremely powerful. Again, it's not exactly *what* you say, but *how* you say it. Good feedback contains concrete and specific details to anchor the student in action, but it also contains an emotional component. Your choice of words communicates your respect, support and positive regard for the student.

Instead of saying, "I can't hear a word you're saying," go with "I can hear your voice so much better when you lift your chin and speak up like that. Then your passion in the speech really comes through."

Instead of saying, "This painting is just a mess," you could say, "I don't think your attempt to bring these elements together has really worked this time, and I have a feeling you didn't fully convey your meaning with your use of color here."

Rather than saying, "The reason you keep injuring yourself is because of your grip on the bat," you could say something like, "What do you think is the effect of holding your bat like that? What do you think would happen if you tried holding it a little higher up?"

Feedback is not the same as **advice**, and it's not the same as **evaluation**. To simply pronounce something good or bad doesn't actually help your student learn or improve. Think about your role in giving feedback as a facilitator of a natural process in life—i.e. we act, our actions have results, and if we want to learn we'd better notice these results and adjust accordingly. Draw attention to the effect of your student's actions, and relate it to the goal. Done *continuously and consistently*, your student is given ample opportunity to actually dig into the material and refine their understanding and their skill. When in doubt, favor feedback over teaching (i.e., the integrative approach to pedagogy).

To check your own skill at providing feedback, regularly ask yourself the following questions:

    a. Does my feedback refer to the goal? Feedback is more focused when it can basically answer the question, does the action I'm evaluating bring the student closer to or further from their stated goal? (Again we see why it's so important to have clearly stated goals in learning. Sometimes, simply reminding your student of the bigger aim is enough of a course correction.)

b. Is your feedback specific, concrete and actionable? Have you given guidance or observations that the student can genuinely do something with? For example, it's no use criticizing your student for not performing beyond what they are genuinely capable of. Keep judgments, assumptions and expectations out of feedback and look at plain, neutral facts, and precisely what to *do* given the feedback.

c. Is your feedback appropriate for your unique student? Feedback is communication, and communication fails if it's not received properly. Are you speaking in a way that is understandable for your student?

d. Does your feedback contain meaningful information on the task, the process, or the performance? In other words, are you offering information which genuinely provides insight and a learning opportunity?

Good feedback:

- is clear, purposeful, meaningful and compatible with prior knowledge
- is focused on the learning intention and success criteria
- occurs *as* students are doing the learning; therefore, verbal feedback is much more effective than written
- provides information on how and why the student has or has not met the criteria
- provides strategies for improvement

According to John Hattie, a prominent education researcher, feedback is useful when it addresses the fundamental questions of "where am I going?", "how am I going?" and "where to next?" These questions are powerful as they reduce the gap between where the student is, and where they are meant to be, in reference to their learning goals. Another form of powerful feedback is that sought by the teacher—where students show the teacher what they have learned (formative assessment).

As part of our explicit teaching culture, teachers regularly provide instructive feedback during the "we do" and "you do" phases. Importantly, explicit instruction often emphasizes the positive function of errors—when teachers make immediate corrections to ensure achievement of learning goals. This type of "error training" can lead to higher performance in classrooms if the teacher has created a safe environment in which students are comfortable in taking risks.

Teachers also use student assessment data, and seek feedback from students in lesson plenaries, as a source of feedback on the effectiveness of their teaching practice. Feedback is also sought from students in our 360-degree performance improvement process.

In the 2017 IPS Review Findings, the reviewers stated: "Discussions with student leaders showed that the setting of achievement goals and the ongoing provision of feedback from teachers about their performance was having a powerful and positive impact on their learning."

Takeaways

- Students will only learn when they are motivated, so it's a teacher's duty to establish a learning environment that supports this motivation.
- Humans take action according to their appraisal of the level of effort required, its likely outcome, and the perceived desirability of that outcome. Teachers can motivate students by increasing the perceived value of the learning goal and its process, as well as boosting expectation of a positive outcome without undermining intrinsic motivation.
- Gamification is an approach where gaming elements are brought into non-gaming contexts, like learning. Teachers can use "level-up" scaffolding, put the "player" in control of play, encourage strategic collaboration, and make sure that the student not only receives immediate feedback for every action, but that their play is always guided by a well-understood purpose and expectation of the "rules."
- Academic buoyancy is something that teachers should always encourage in students, and this consists of composure, confidence, coordination, commitment, and control. With a mindset that fosters the development of these traits, the difficult

aspects of learning are overcome and mastered as surely as the material itself.

- Productive failure is the perspective that failure itself is a valuable teacher, and can enhance understanding and mastery more than success can. Teachers can model an optimal attitude to failure—i.e. that it is normal, manageable and indeed useful.

- Good teachers should create a learning atmosphere free from judgment. This means disconnecting performance from the student's self-worth or identity, so that failure and mistakes are not perceived as threatening or humiliating. When a teacher models nonjudgment, a student feels safe to explore, experiment and make purposeful mistakes on their learning journey.

- Feedback is a vital part of the student environment. Good feedback is concrete, specific to the goal in question, timely, meaningful, relevant and understandable to the student, and comes with clear and realistic steps for next actions. It is not judgment, advice, praise or criticism without meaningful elaboration on the learning process itself.

CHAPTER 1. LESSONS FROM THE SCIENCE OF PEDAGOGY

- We can draw on the five most common pedagogical approaches to become better teachers, whether that's inside the classroom or in more informal contexts.
- The constructivist approach is about building up knowledge and skill from information that is already known to the student. You help them "construct" new knowledge by relating everything to this set of existing knowledge in order to connect two different concepts.
- The integrative approach focuses on making lessons practical and applicable in the real world. The more relevant and contextual new information is, the more likely students are to retain it.
- The collaborative approach uses the strengths of group collaboration between students to support learning. You rely on

students within the group to teach each other by exposing them to unique viewpoints and knowledge that everyone has.

- The inquiry-based approach is about directing learning by asking the student to devise a question, a method for arriving at an answer, the answer, or some combination of these three.

- The reflective approach is about tailoring the teaching methods used to best fit the student in front of you, regularly taking time to appraise what works and what doesn't.

- The brain is not a machine. Cognitive load theory tells us that as the brain's power is limited, we need to think strategically and reduce load while maximizing learning. This can be done in a variety of ways that respect rather than push against the brain's natural learning processes. Some strategies involve keeping your material focused on particular topics, repeating information as much as you can, and appealing to the senses in ways that pique attention.

- Scaffolding is the principle of making small, incremental improvements and building bigger concepts or skills from smaller, simpler ones. This can be summarized as "I do, we do, you do" to show how the teacher gradually hands over control and mastery to the student.

CHAPTER 2. SEEING THE LANDSCAPE

- Excellent teachers know how to "see the landscape" ahead of them, and their understanding of the field of learning allows them to set goals and parameters, prioritize and frame tasks, and gauge their students' current understanding.
- Concept maps are simplified models of more complex material that make clear the connections between different ideas. Concept maps can be drawn by both student and teacher to gauge knowledge gaps, plan lessons, learn those lessons, and assess the effectiveness of that learning.
- Concept maps consist of simplified chunks or pieces of information arranged to highlight the relationships or connections between them. A good concept map is relevant, simple, accurate and draws on existing mental models and knowledge.
- Once you've identified what your student already knows, the next step is planning how to utilize that. In some cases, this will be easy in that you only need to teach them certain concepts that will help them

understand the topic you wanted to teach them in the first place. However, you could also combine the usage of concept-based maps with an inquiry-based approach and problematize what students already know in order to make them curious and eager to learn more.

- The Feynman technique is a "bigger picture" technique that allows both teacher and student to identify their own mental blind spots. First, identify the concept in question, then write down an explanation of it in plain English, then identify any areas where the explanation fails or where data is missing. Then, use the power of analogy to fill in the gaps, i.e. use pre-existing mental models to better understand new material.

- Analogies can aid learning because they connect old knowledge with new. Analogies can be Antonyms, Types, or Characteristics, each expressing the qualities of a new concept in terms of already understood concepts. Analogies are best when as many are used as possible, and they encourage higher-order abstract thinking.

CHAPTER 3. THE NUTS AND BOLTS

- There are a range of practical methods to help on the learning journey. The SQ3R method is a way to shape the learning process, via Survey (gain an overview of the material), Question (develop deeper understanding by asking questions to direct your learning), Read (active, careful intake of the material or information), Recite (drill what has been learnt to organize and cement it in your mind) and Review (assess your progress as compared to the start, and according to your overall goals).
- Bloom's taxonomy explains that mastery is cumulative, and proceeds through levels of deepening understanding. These are Remember, Understand, Apply, Analyze, Evaluate, and Create. Each of these levels of engagement depends on mastery of the previous level. As a teacher, you can shape progressive challenge by bearing these stages in mind.
- Spaced repetition or distributed practice is a way to strengthen memory and recall. The idea is to recite or review material at frequent intervals spaced over as long a period as possible, rather than "cramming" all at once, which is less effective. The key is consistency and spaced-out practice, which allows students to practice recall itself.

- The Cornell Method of note-taking teaches your student to take natural notes, but then later distill key themes and points from those notes and then summarize their main findings, essentially generating a concept map of the material. This improves not only retention but depth understanding.
- Finally, purposeful annotation is something done during reading, but in reality occurs before, during and after reading. Reading should be active and directed; you need to know beforehand why you are reading and what you intend to do with the information after you've read. This knowledge primes and focuses reading, and makes it easier to choose annotation methods (highlighting, notes, symbols, etc.) that work in context.

CHAPTER 4. ADVANCED TECHNIQUES

- Once you've mastered the more straightforward teaching techniques, you might like to try more advanced methods. PBL or problem-based learning, for example, is an integrative approach where students are presented with a problem and guided to find the solution for themselves, gaining deeper understanding. PBL is excellent for giving students responsibility for their own learning, and creates realistic, applicable and memorable lessons.

- The Socratic method is another depth approach that rests on strategic inquiry. Questions can be used to unearth assumptions and bias, to probe for richer understanding, to flesh out perspectives, explore consequences and implications, examine an argument's deeper rationale, or even look more closely at the question itself.

- The key to the Socratic approach is asking questions so that your interlocutor or student has enough room to express their opinion. Once you've got them to reveal what they think, probe them further by either asking for clarifications, elaborating on something they glossed over, or problematizing something they said. These tactics force students to learn and understand new concepts by having gaps in their knowledge exposed.

- Critical thinking is a great approach for more advanced concepts, as it encourages meta-cognition about both the quality of one's thoughts and the material and learning process itself. Critical thinking is characterized by an attitude of open-mindedness, and a tolerance for ambiguity or uncertainty that takes nothing for granted. Often, it involves following an inquiry-based approach wherein you're continuously asking your students questions that challenge their beliefs in ways that stimulate discussion and learning.

- Other advanced techniques can use group work to aid learning (for example student-teacher tasks, "pair and share," debate or student observation) or relevant visual materials (such as relationship maps, flowcharts, Venn diagrams or storyboards).

- All these more advanced techniques require the student to be proactive in their learning, and they allow the teacher to not only gauge understanding but offer useful feedback.

CHAPTER 5. THE STUDENT ENVIRONMENT

- Students will only learn when they are motivated, so it's a teacher's duty to establish a learning environment that supports this motivation.

- Humans take action according to their appraisal of the level of effort required, its likely outcome, and the perceived desirability of that outcome. Teachers can motivate students by increasing the perceived value of the learning goal and its process, as well as boosting expectation of a positive outcome without undermining intrinsic motivation.

- Gamification is an approach where gaming elements are brought into non-gaming contexts, like learning. Teachers can use "level-up" scaffolding, put the "player" in control of play, encourage strategic collaboration, and make sure that the student not only receives immediate feedback for every action, but that their play is always guided by a well-understood purpose and expectation of the "rules."

- Academic buoyancy is something that teachers should always encourage in students, and this consists of composure, confidence, coordination, commitment, and control. With a mindset that fosters the development of these traits, the difficult aspects of learning are overcome and mastered as surely as the material itself.

- Productive failure is the perspective that failure itself is a valuable teacher, and can enhance understanding and mastery more than success can. Teachers can model an optimal attitude to failure—i.e. that it is normal, manageable and indeed useful.

- Good teachers should create a learning atmosphere free from judgment. This means disconnecting performance from the student's self-worth or identity, so that failure and mistakes are not perceived as threatening or humiliating. When a teacher models nonjudgment, a student feels safe to explore, experiment and make purposeful mistakes on their learning journey.

- Feedback is a vital part of the student environment. Good feedback is concrete, specific to the goal in question, timely, meaningful, relevant and understandable to the student, and comes with clear and realistic steps for next actions. It is not judgment, advice, praise or criticism without meaningful elaboration on the learning process itself.

Made in the USA
Las Vegas, NV
04 November 2024

11108473R10125